HIGHLIGHTS OF
TEMPLAR HISTORY

WILLIAM MOSELEY BRO....

Includes the Templar Constitution and Abbreviated By-Laws
By Simeon B. Chase

Prepared for the Committee on Templar History
of the
GRAND ENCAMPMENT, KNIGHTS TEMPLAR
UNITED STATES OF AMERICA

Second Edition

With 16 Illustrations

THE BOOK TREE
SAN DIEGO, CALIFORNIA

First published 1944
Grand Encampment of Knights Templar
United States of America

Constitution & By-Laws
Amended version, 1868

ISBN 1-58509-230-4

Cover layout & design
Lee Berube

Printed on Acid-Free Paper
in the United States of America

Published by
The Book Tree
P O Box 16476
San Diego, CA 92176
www.thebooktree.com

We provide fascinating and educational products to help awaken the public to new ideas and information that would not be available otherwise.
Call 1 (800) 700-8733 for our *FREE BOOK TREE CATALOG*.

THE ISLAND OF MALTA
(From an old map now in possession of the Grand Encampment, U. S. A.)

FOREWARD TO SECOND EDITION

There are a number of revealing books on the Knights Templar, yet few are written from an insiders point of view. This book was originally released by the Grand Encampment of Knights Templar, United States of America, after seven years of historical research by an assigned committee. The research had not been entirely finished due to World War II, but this book still provides a wealth of accurate knowledge due to their efforts.

The author, William Moseley Brown, was part of that committee and their purpose was to provide the Templars with an accurate history of their organization. It was for members only and much of the information cannot be found elsewhere. As one will see from the original Foreward (to follow), written by the Grand Master himself, this book was the first attempt by this organization to provide their members with an authentic and official history. It seems that an expanded version of this work was desired, but never realized.

Some of the chapters include The Place of Templary in the Masonic System, Religious and Military Orders, Theories of Masonic Templar Origins, and Templar Rituals. Interesting connections are explored including the link between the ancient Templars and the modern Masonic Knights Templar, plus the connections between the Templars and the Knights of Malta.

We have added additional information to this book that is extremely important and rare—the Templar's Constitution and Abbreviated By-Laws. The complete *Digest of the Laws, Decisions, Rules and Usages of the Independent Order of Good Templars* was over 420 pages thick and its last known date of publication was the tenth edition from 1874. As of this writing there are no modern editions of this digest available, so we wish to provide a small but important part of it as a service to members and potential members of the Order, or for those who simply desire a better knowledge of the inner workings of the Templars.

These two works, combined together, will hopefully shed new light on an interesting and sometimes mysterious organization.

Paul Tice

CONTENTS

PAGE

Foreword 6

Preface 7

Introduction 9

Chapter I—The Place of Templary in the Masonic System 11

Chapter II—Religious and Military Orders................ 15

Chapter III—The Monastic Military Orders................ 22

Chapter IV—Theories Connecting Chivalric Freemasonry with the Medieval Order of Knights Templar 35

Chapter V—Theories of Masonic Templar Origins.. 40

Chapter VI—Templar Rituals 62

Appendix—Calendar of Templar Events in the U. S. A. (1769-1816) 68

FOREWORD

THE present work represents the first attempt of the Grand Encampment of Knights Templar to compile and publish for general distribution among its members an authentic and official statement covering any of the phases of the magnificent and inspiring history of the ancient Templars and their spiritual heirs, the Masonic Knights Templar. It comes at a time when the principles of Templar Masonry are sorely needed in the reconstruction of the social and economic institutions of mankind. Certainly there has been no more opportune moment for the release of such a publication in the past quarter of a century.

The book, as its name implies, does not attempt a complete historical statement on any of the subjects, of which it treats. It is merely a forerunner, a harbinger, so to speak, of what it is hoped the Grand Encampment will be able to undertake in the way of a complete history of Templary from its beginnings when peace once more returns to the world. It is believed, that the material contained herein is reliable and will stand the test of minute scrutiny by scholars and laymen as well. The treatment of the material is in popular style and should make the book, therefore, acceptable to the rank and file of Knights Templar throughout the country. The illustrations add much to the book's attractiveness. It should be read, in my opinion, by every Templar in the United States and I hope, that the very reasonable price, at which the book will be made available, will do much to accomplish this end.

It is with pleasure that I commend this publication to every American Templar.

CHARLES NOAH ORR,
M. E. Grand Master, Grand Encampment
of Knights Templar of the U. S. A.

PREFACE

THIS little volume is presented as the first fruit of the researches of the Committee on Templar History authorized by the Grand Encampment of Knights Templar, U. S. A., in 1937. Much of the material herein contained was presented to Grand Encampment in the committee's reports for 1940 and 1943 and a large part of the narrative section of the book appeared in more than thirty Masonic magazines during the past two or three years. It is believed that the statements made are based upon accurate historical information and readers are invited to correspond with the committee concerning any errors found in the book.

The purpose of the present treatise is threefold: first, to stimulate interest among Knights Templar in particular and Freemasons in general in the historic facts which form the background of modern Templar Masonry; second, to assist in informing the constituency of our Order as to its ancestry and lineage; and third, to aid in preparing the way for the larger work, which is planned by Grand Encampment when circumstances make its publication feasible.

Grateful acknowledgment is made for valuable assistance rendered by the following in the preparation of this work: Claud Keltner for his invaluable researches extending over a period of many months and terminated before their completion because of war conditions; Ward K. St. Clair, P. C., for most of the discussion of Templar rituals; James Fairbairn Smith, P. C., for valuable suggestions and the use of many of the cuts used in the book; George Hay Kain, P. G. C., for reading the proofs and making a number of suggestions for improving the arrangement of the material; and the late lamented Mark Norris, P. G. M., for his untiring zeal and interest in the entire program of preparing and publishing a definite history of Masonic

Templary. Our thanks are also due to Grand Master Charles N. Orr and Grand Recorder Adrian Hamersly for their helpful and constructive criticisms throughout the progress of the committee's efforts in connection with the present volume.

If the objectives set forth above shall be achieved in some small measure, we shall feel more than repaid for this modest beginning of an official and authentic history of Templary.

"Non nobis, Domine, non nobis, sed nomini tuo da gloriam."

ANDREW D. AGNEW, P. G. M., Chmn.
CHALMERS L. PANCOAST, P. G. C.
WM. MOSELEY BROWN, P. G. C.
Committee on Templar History.

INTRODUCTION

NOT SINCE the first half of the last century has the Grand Encampment of Knights Templar, U. S. A., given so much thought to Templar history as in the last ten years. In fact, on only one previous occasion was any serious attempt made to prepare a complete and authentic history under the auspices of the Grand Encampment. For many reasons, this attempt almost died a-borning, chiefly (as it appears from the records of the period) because no adequate and detailed program had been worked out for handling the tremendous undertaking involved. This was nearly a century ago.

At the 1937 Triennial, Grand Master Andrew D. Agnew recommended the appointment of a special committee to study the whole matter and to report its findings to Grand Encampment before the conclusion of that conclave. This committee reported favorably and recommended the appointment of a Committee on Templar History to function during the interim and to make recommendations to the next Triennial. A modest amount was made available for preliminary researches to be conducted by this committee. The investigations conducted during the three-year period proved so encouraging in their results, that the committee recommended in 1940, that it be continued with the authority to carry on its work even more intensively than before. The recommendation was approved unanimously by Grand Encampment and the previous program of study and research on a moderate but comprehensive scale was continued.

With the outbreak of the war in 1939 and especially after the entry of the United States into the war in December, 1941, the committee decided to devote its attention primarily to the American scene, so to speak. Therefore, the past four years have been devoted to preparing histories of Templary in all the jurisdictions in our own country with the aid of outstanding authorities in the respective states. As soon as practicable after the present war has been con- ·cluded, it is hoped that investigations abroad may be started, which will give ultimately the answer to the age-old question as to whether or not there is an organic connection between Masonic Templary and the famed heroes of the Crusades.

Certainly there will be an important rôle for Masonry and Templary in world reconstruction after the present con- flict is over. Not the least contribution, which we can make as Knights Templar to the coming generations, is to gain a knowledge of our antecedents and to interpret our back- ground in terms of modern social and individual problems. If we can build a world according to the plans, which the ancient Templars developed but which, unfortunately, they were prevented from carrying out, we may perhaps recap- ture their spirit and zeal and find Jerusalem, the holy city, actually established among the children of men. Then, in- deed, will the cry of the Crusaders take on a new meaning: "Deus vult!" "It is the will of God!"

So mote it be!

WILLIAM MOSELEY BROWN

Fort Monmouth, New Jersey
September, 1943

CHAPTER I

THE PLACE OF TEMPLARY IN THE MASONIC SYSTEM

FREEMASONRY is a system of ethics wherein moral precepts are taught by lessons based on the allegorical use of the operative craftsman's tools. These lessons, designed to instruct the candidate in the allegorical use of the tools to prepare him as the symbolic material for the edifice acceptable to the Supreme Architect of the Universe, are distributed throughout a series of Degrees and Orders. Symbolic Freemasonry instructs the candidate in the allegorical use of the operative craftsman's tools to prepare the symbolic stone in a manner suitable for use in the edifice designed by the Supreme Architect. Capitular and Cryptic Freemasonry instruct the candidate in the allegorical use of certain additional tools of the operative craftsman, how to fit the symbolic stone into the edifice, and, finally, how to restore the edifice once it has been destroyed or allowed to fall into decay. Chivalric Freemasonry instructs the candidate in the allegorical use of the weapons and the discharge of the duties of knighthood whereby the moral edifice, built and restored in Symbolic, Capitular and Cryptic Freemasonry, can be defended and beautified by the precepts of Christianity.

The system of ethics taught in Freemasonry is as old as civilization itself, but organized Freemasonry is the result of man's desire to perpetuate the system found so acceptable through the long centuries since the dawn of time. Organized Freemasonry, as it is found throughout the world today, developed during the closing decades of the sixteenth century, gradually crystallized in the seventeenth, and came into fully organized form in the eighteenth century. During the eighteenth and nineteenth centuries able men, well schooled in the philosophy of Freemasonry, enlarged upon the lessons based on allegorical illustrations until they developed a complete system of rules for ethical conduct in the modern world. As the lessons were improved, these men became aware of the necessity of adding other lessons to complete the system. This was accomplished by adding other Degrees and Orders to those which were worked as a part of the original operative system. Chivalric Freemasonry is the result of the efforts of those Freemasons, who desired to formulate a Masonic Philosophy based upon the principles of Christianity.

Lessons of Templar Masonry

Thus, Chivalric Freemasonry conforms to a pattern of ethical conduct exemplified by those associations of soldier-friars who defended the Holy City, Jerusalem (the perpetual symbol of Christianity), which contained the edifice which is symbolically constructed and restored in Symbolic, Capitular and Cryptic Freemasonry. Chivalric Freemasonry consists at present of four Orders: the Order of the Red Cross, the Order of the Mediterranean Pass, the Order of Malta, and the Order of the Temple. The allegorical illustrations used in Chivalric Freemasonry, with the exception of those taught in the Order of the Red Cross, are based on the rules, duties and achievements of the two great religious and military orders of the Temple and of St. John, known respectively as the Knights Templar and the Knights Hospitaller. Some of the lessons of Chivalric Freemasonry taught by allegorical illustrations are:

1. Veneration for and adherence to the Ancient Landmarks of Freemasonry.
2. Truth is the wisdom, strength, beauty, power and majesty which will prevail over all obstacles.
3. Pilgrimage and penance are necessary for admission to the privileges of Christian Knighthood.
4. Humility is a fundamental virtue of Christian Knighthood.
5. The mystic swords of Faith, Hope and Charity, tempered with Justice, Fortitude and Mercy, will

defend and vindicate the honor of all Knights
of the Order.

6. Christian Knights will wield their mystic swords
   in the defense of innocent maidens, destitute
   widows, helpless orphans, and the Christian religion.

7. Faith in the deity of Jesus of Nazareth as shown
   by his birth, life, death, resurrection, and ascen-
   sion.

8. Belief in the mortality of the body and the im-
   mortality of the soul.

9. Inviolability of the engagements entered into by
   the Templar.

10. Respect for and adherence to the principles estab-
    lished by legal and constitutional government.

Various interpretations based on historical evidence have
been advanced to show that Chivalric Freemasonry is the
lineal descendant of the religious and military orders of the
Knights Templar and the Knights Hospitaller. While there
may be a reasonable basis for doubting this theory, it cannot
be denied that Chivalric Freemasonry has preserved the
traditions of those great Orders in the allegorical lessons
used to teach the lessons of Chivalric Freemasonry. Although many writers have advanced partial proof of this
continued existence after the suppression of the Templars
in 1314, none has been able to trace the intervening and
connecting events with historical accuracy.

Discovering the "Connecting Link"

One of the highly important objectives of present day
students of Templar history is the determination of whether
or not there is an organic connection between the ancient
Templars and the modern Masonic Knights Templar. This
is a most intriguing problem and it can be answered satis-
factorily only after all the available evidence has been
gathered and collated.

On this subject historians have arrayed themselves into
two camps, which may be designated for our present pur-

poses as the "pros" and the "cons." The former hold that there is an organic connection and have suggested six possible avenues by which the organic connection might have occurred:

1. The Templars who fled to Scotland, joining their comrades there and fighting under Bruce, eventually being constituted into a new order.
2. The Templars who fled to Sweden, joining with those under Pierre d'Aumont, and constituting a new order, which flowered as the "Rite of Strict Observance."
3. The Templars who escaped and remained in France, joined others under John Marc Larmenius, and continued the Order there.
4. The Templars in Portugal, who entered the Order created by Dion II, known as the Order of Christ.
5. The Templars in England, who kept the Order alive as a fraternal organization until it became a part of the system of Freemasonry.
6. The Templars, who entered the Order of St. John, and who perpetuated the ritual and observances in the Order, and consequently dominated the Order of St. John.

Those who contend that there was no connection between the two orders base their contentions mainly upon the following:

1. That the Papal Bull was absolute and consequently the ban of excommunication would have prevented the Templars from maintaining the Order.
2. That the Papal Bull for the same reason would have prevented the Templars from entering other orders as Templars.
3. The lack of historical evidence of an Order called the Templars during the long period between the active existence of the two orders (more than three centuries).

CHAPTER II

RELIGIOUS AND MILITARY ORDERS

A BRIEF REVIEW of the history of the religious and military orders of Knights Templar and Knights Hospitaller is necessary to establish the connecting links between those orders and the Chivalric Orders of Freemasonry. The religious and military orders of Knights Templar and Knights Hospitaller were developed during the period when the Latin Christians possessed the Holy Land. These orders performed duties which could not be accomplished by the government of the Latin Kingdom of Jerusalem, which was founded after the Christian armies conquered that city as the consummation of the First Crusade.

The Crusades

Historians have called that series of Holy Wars waged by the Latin Christians for the possession of the Holy Land the Crusades. One of the contributing causes for this series of wars was a desire to make pilgrimages to the Holy Places safe for all desiring to undertake them.

As the Roman Empire slowly declined, Christianity gained in strength and numbers until it had become the universal religion of the Mediterranean World at the time that the barbarian invaders conquered nearly all of the Empire. Christianity, when it was introduced into the Roman Empire, was an urban religion teaching individual ethical conduct based on the teachings of Jesus of Nazareth. Christianity taught the spiritual manifestation of Deity in human experience whereas paganism contented itself largely with physical manifestations. The Roman philosophers maintained that the universe was held together by law whereas Christianity maintained that it was bound together by Deity.

After their conversion to Christianity, the barbarian invaders insisted upon visible manifestations similar to those exhibited by their discarded pagan gods. Primarily rural in

their customs the barbarians were accustomed to manifestations displayed by their pagan gods in relation to their crops,
hunting, warfare, and other tasks incident to daily life. The
search for visible manifestations in Christianity was satisfied
by the relics of the Christian martyrs and apostles. Churches
possessing one of these relics became the centers of attrac-
tion to these newly converted people. They travelled long
distances to behold the miracles wrought by them. Naturally, the most valuable relics were in Palestine where Jesus
of Nazareth had lived and where the disciples had begun
their preaching.

Gradually journeys to the shrines of Christendom assumed an organized form of travel along well-defined routes.
Primarily the religious purpose of a pilgrimage was to secure
the remission of punishment for sin but it served also to
strengthen the faith of those newly converted to Christianity. Pilgrims were easily distinguished by their distinctive
garb, which consisted of a hood and cape, a low-crowned
hat turned up in front and fastened at the throat by strings,
a staff, a water bottle and pilgrim's scrip. Long pilgrimages
were usually effected in large groups under the leadership
of a competent Church official. Guide books, necessities,
and information were furnished by those who derived a
profit from assisting and conducting pilgrimages.

Beginnings of the Crusades

No serious obstacle was erected by the Mohammedan
conquerors of the Holy Land until the Turkoman chieftain,
Torgul Beg, conquered Jerusalem in 1076. The fierce des-
ert raiders who overran Palestine began to harass and de-
stroy the Christian pilgrims. The sufferings of the pilgrims,
therefore, became the immediate concern of the church.
Two decades passed before an effective solution presented
itself because the Church was engaged in a serious struggle
with the Empire in the West. Pope Urban II, in 1095,
called a council to meet at Clermont to consider the problems confronting the Church and Christiandom. At the con-

clusion of the Council of Clermont, Urban preached a sermon exhorting the Christians to undertake a Holy War for the recovery of Jerusalem and the Holy Places from the infidel Turks. Hundreds immediately took the cross signifying their intention to participate in the Holy War.

Roused by the fervent exhortation of itinerant preachers, thousands started on the long journey with no other knowledge than the name of the Holy City, Jerusalem, on their lips. This more or less abortive movement, called the People's Crusade, under the leadership of Peter the Hermit, Walter the Penniless, and others, was not sufficiently organized to hope for success. Zeal for the cause could not save the undisciplined people who took part in it from the hardships and dangers of the long march to Constantinople. The bones of thousands were left bleaching along the Old Pilgrim's Road and a few thousands, who reached Constantinople, were cut to pieces as soon as they crossed into Asia Minor.

In August, 1096, the great organized armies of the First Crusade assembled for the long march to Jerusalem. Under the wise and competent leadership of Aldehmar du Puy, the Papal legate, every possible precaution had been exercised to prevent the failure of the undertaking. None were accepted who could not furnish equipment and funds necessary for their individual needs during the march of the Christian forces. The organized armies of the First Crusade were led by able leaders who had proved themselves in the many minor wars which had been fought in the West, but which were now ended by the Pope's decree of a Truce of God.

The first army to move was the one composed of the men of Lorraine under the leadership of Godfrey of Bouillon and Baldwin of Flanders. This army began its march on August 15, 1096, choosing the march over the Old Pilgrim's Road to Jerusalem. It reached Constantinople on December 23, 1096. Armies under Hugh de Vermandois,

LEADERS OF THE FIRST CRUSADE

The four leaders of the first real Crusade were Godfrey de Bouillon;
Robert, Duke of Normandy; Robert, Count of Flanders; and Tancred.
It resulted in the capture of Jerusalem in 1099. A previous attempt
which met with failure had been made by Peter the Hermit.

brother of the King of France, Robert of Normandy, Stephen of Blois, and Robert of Flanders, did not fully assemble before Constantinople until May, 1097. Hugh de Vermandois and Robert of Flanders with a few followers reached Constantinople a few days before Godfrey and Baldwin. The Provençals under Raymond of St. Giles, the Count of Toulouse, marching through northern Italy, arrived in front of Constantinople in April, 1097. Normans under Bohemond and Tancred proceeded by sea to Durange and then overland to Constantinople, arriving there early in May, 1097. The Emperor of the East, Alexius Comenius, compelled the Crusaders to take an oath of fealty to him, pledging the restoration of all his lost possessions.

On May 15, 1097, the Crusaders assembled before the walls of Nicaea, which capitulated after a month's siege. On June 29, 1097, the armies marched from Nicaea toward the arid highlands of Asia Minor. Two days later the crusading armies defeated the Moslems in the first pitched battle of the Crusades at Doryleum. Thousands of the Crusaders died of thirst and exhaustion during the march southward over the sultry, arid highlands. Two of the leaders, Baldwin of Flanders and Tancred, with their followers, turned away from the main army of Crusaders for personal adventure and gain which resulted in the capture of Edessa.

After weeks of indecision, the main army suddenly wheeled southward and arrived before the city of Antioch, October 20, 1097. Antioch withstood a siege by the combined might of the crusading armies from October 21, 1097, until the city capitulated, June 3, 1098. As soon as the Crusaders took possession of the city they were in turn besieged by the Moslems. When the spirits of the Crusaders were at the lowest ebb a Provençal cleric, Peter Bartholomew, discovered the lance which had pierced the side of Jesus. This discovery inflamed the Crusaders to redouble their efforts and the Moslems were decisively defeated on June 26, 1098.

Quarrels broke out among the leaders over the division of the spoils and it seemed for a time that the expedition would never resume the march against Jerusalem. After many disputes the main army finally resumed the march toward Jerusalem under the leadership of Raymond of Toulouse. On June 10, 1099, the crusading armies arrived before the Holy City and immediately invested it.

FIRST VIEW OF JERUSALEM
The Crusaders obtained their first view of Jerusalem from the Hill of Emmaus June 10, 1099, and immediately invested it under the leadership of Raymond of Toulouse. They finally stormed into the Holy City July 15, 1099, using as their battle cry: "Jerusalem! Jerusalem!! It is the will of God! It is the will of God!!"

Jerusalem Delivered

Assault after assault failed, but, as the hour of the Crucifixion approached, on the morning of July 15, 1099, the followers of Godfrey of Bouillon broke through the northeast wall. Slowly they fought their way to the center of the city where they met the Crusaders under Raymond, who had broken through the south wall. Riding through the streets which ran with the blood of the infidels ". . . up to the knees of their horses," the Crusaders ". . . came rejoicing, nay for exceeding great joy weeping, to the tomb of our Saviour to adore and give thanks." The soldiers of the Cross had fulfilled the pledge—"Deus Vult!" "It is the will of God!"

After a period of rejoicing, the Crusaders met to select one of their leaders to rule the conquered lands. They chose Godfrey of Bouillon. Godfrey refused to wear a crown of gold where Jesus had worn a crown of thorns, but chose to be called *Baron and Defender of the Holy Sepulchre* instead of *King of Jerusalem*. Godfrey died within the year and Baldwin, his brother, was chosen as ruler. Under his patient conciliatory rule the frontiers were strengthened, conquests consolidated, and law established through the realm. Baldwin I died in 1118 and was succeeded by his nephew, Baldwin de Bourge, as Baldwin II. Under Baldwin II the conquests were finally consolidated and the Latin Kingdom of Jerusalem reached its greatest territorial limits.

Three remarkable organizations developed during the occupation of the Holy Land by the Latin Christians, namely, the Knights Templar, the Knights Hospitaller, and the Teutonic Knights. Each of these organizations rendered valuable military service to the Latin Kingdom of Jerusalem and played a conspicuous rôle in all the Crusades except the First and the Fourth. Although originally designed to render specific secular service, they later assumed the character of monastic brotherhoods. A brief history of these orders is given in the following chapters.

CHAPTER III

THE MONASTIC MILITARY ORDERS

THE THREE organizations, which developed during the occupation of the Holy Land by the Latin Christians, were the Knights Templar, the Knights Hospitaller, and the Teutonic Knights. A brief summary of the essential facts regarding each order is here presented.

1. The Templars

The most powerful and spectacular of these orders was the Knights Templar, *Pauperes Comilitiones Christi Templique Solomonici* (Poor Fellow-Soldiers of Christ and the Temple of Solomon). Many of the circumstances which led to the formation of this Order escaped the notice of contemporary chroniclers. The Order was organized by eight knights under the leadership of a Burgundian knight, Hugh of Payen, in 1118. Soon the Order attracted the attention of Baldwin II, King of Jerusalem, who sanctioned it and assigned it quarters in a building on the site once occupied by King Solomon's Temple.

Baldwin II recognized the importance of securing ecclesiastical sanction for the newly formed Order. Consequently, he dispatched two members of the Order to Europe. These knights enlisted the support of Bernard, Abbot of Clairvaux, the most powerful churchman in the West. Soon afterward, Hugh and other members of the Order came to Europe to assist. Ecclesiastical sanction was granted at the Council of Troyes in 1128. This sanction gave to the Order the authority needed to secure recruits and financial assistance in the west for activities in the Holy Land.

Originally, the Order's principal objective was the protection of pilgrims on their way to worship at the Sepulchre of Jesus in Jerusalem. The original members assumed the vows of chastity, poverty, and obedience. As the membership and properties increased, it became necessary to prepare an elaborate *Rule* of conduct for the Order. Nearly every activity of the individual Templar was governed by a section of the *Rule*. Prayers at stipulated times were commanded of each Templar whether he was in the House or on duty in the field. Only the Master of the house could excuse a member from participation in divine service. Some sacred book was read during each of the two meals permitted daily. Each knight was required to keep himself and his equipment ready for instant service in the field.

In addition to their very plain armor, the knights wore a linen or woolen surplice. This garment was white to remind them that they had turned away from the dark life. Worn garments were returned to the drapier, the officer in charge of clothing, only when they were no longer fit for use. The only great coats permitted were made from the skins of lambs or goats. The chaplains of the Order were the only clerics in the whole ecclesiastical system permitted to wear white garments.

No knight was permitted to have more than three mounts. Horses were generally very carefully guarded and their loss counted a great misfortune. A record was kept in which was entered not only the price but also a description of each horse purchased by or given to the Order.

Administration of the Order

For the administration of affairs of the Order, the territory in which it held possessions was divided into provinces. These provinces in the east were Jerusalem, Antioch, Tripoli, and Greece; in the west they were France, England, Germany and Hungary, Portugal, Aragon, Castille, Upper and Central Italy, and Apulia and Sicily. Jerusalem ranked first among the provinces as it was the residence of the Grand Master. The Grand Master's headquarters were first in the Temple in Jerusalem, but after 1187, when the city fell to Saladin, they were transferred to Castle Pilgrim

at Acre. The chief officer of the province was the Grand
Preceptor or Grand Prior. Under Grand Preceptors were
the Preceptors, who had jurisdiction over several houses
or preceptories within a province. Over each preceptory
or house was a Commander. The governing body of the
Order was the Chapter. Each province had a Chapter to
administer its affairs. This Chapter was composed of the

SAINT-JEAN D'ACRE, SYRIA

When Acre, which was the last stronghold of the Knights Templar and
the Knights Hospitaller, fell in May, 1291, the Hospitallers, like the Templars, retired to the Island of Cyprus. Their influence increased and their
wealth grew by leaps and bounds. They later moved to Rhodes and in
1523 to Crete. In 1530 they came into possession of Malta, by deed of
gift from Charles V.

Grand Preceptor, Preceptors, Commanders, and other principal officers residing in the province. Matters of policy,
affecting the Order only in the east, were determined in a
Grand Chapter composed of the Grand Preceptors of the
provinces of the east. A similar Grand Chapter was held
in the west. A General Grand Chapter, composed of all
the Grand Preceptors and principal officers, was held at
the residence of the Grand Master to decide all important

policies affecting the entire Order.   Usually the custom was to hold a Grand Chapter for each province once yearly, and other Chapters as the occasion required.   As a liaison between the Grand Master and the distant provinces were officers, styled Visitors General, appointed to inspect and supervise the affairs of the Order.   The Visitor General reported his activities to the Grand Master, as well as anything of interest observed during a tour of inspection.   The Visitor General was given authority to dismiss officers found unworthy, revise the local regulations, issue orders for the conduct of the Order in the province, and enforce all regulations of the Order.

As the wealth of the Order increased, the necessity for strict observance of the original tenets became more pronounced.   Kings and cardinals were willing to assist in the raising of men and wealth for the conflict in the east, but reluctant to aid in the building up of a powerful organization within their own territories.   In spite of its frequent clashes with the nobles of the west, the Order became so firmly entrenched that it often controlled the policy of an entire kingdom.   In many kingdoms Templars became men of affairs.   Often they were selected as almoners for the Kings of England and France.

By acting as a depository for the wealth of any person, who desired such services, the Templars became largely the bankers of Europe.   In order to facilitate the transfer of money, the Templars issued letters of credit and deposit, which were paid in full when presented for payment at any of the houses of the Order.

As its influence and wealth increased, admission into the Order became restricted. Novitiates were required to answer questions not previously asked.   They were asked, for example: "Do you swear to God and our Lady Mary that during all the days of your life you will with strength and power given you by God, fight for the Holy Land of Jerusalem and assist in holding and protecting the possessions of the

Christians to the best of your ability?" Novitiates were required to answer, "Yes sir, if God pleases." They were also asked if they would live in chastity, obey the Master, observe the rules of the Order, protect all Christians, live in poverty, serve in any land to which they were sent, and if they were willing to become servants of God.

ST. BERNARD PREACHES THE SECOND CRUSADE

St. Bernard, Abbot of Clairvaux, urging Crusaders on to make a second attempt to win the Holy Land. He was one of the most eminent churchmen of the middle ages. In 1128, through his influence, the Order of Knights Templar was confirmed by the Council of Troyes; and he is said to have composed the rules which afterwards governed the Order. In exhorting the Knights he said: "Illustrious knights, generous defenders of the Cross, remember the example of your fathers who conquered Jerusalem, and whose names are inscribed in heaven; abandon, then, the things which perish to gather eternal palms, and conquer a kingdom which has no end."

The Templars Leave Palestine

As the Christian forces fell back in Palestine, the Templars retired with them until, at last, only Acre remained in the hands of the Latin Christians. When Acre fell, the

Templars retired to Cyprus, which they had purchased from Richard the Lion Heart. They had one more day of glory when, in 1299, they again entered the Holy City and worshipped at the Holy Sepulchre.

The Templars were the greatest professional soldiers of their day. Their apparent arrogance was due not so much to their wealth as to their pride in their professional ability as soldiers. Although the losses suffered by the Order were enormous during two centuries of almost constant warfare in the Holy Land, the Order, because of the reputation of its members as soldiers, attracted a constant stream of recruits from the west.

After the Templars retired to Cyprus, the Grand Master, Jacques de Molay, tried in vain to arouse the monarchs of Europe and the Pope to undertake a new Crusade. Unfortunately for the Order, the church was engaged in struggles with the secular rulers of Germany and France. Philip IV, King of France, was able to secure the election of a French Cardinal as Pope Clement V. Under the pretense of trying to unite the forces of Christiandom in a new Crusade, Clement invited the Grand Master of the Templars and the Grand Master of the Hospitallers to Paris for a conference. The Grand Master of the Hospitallers declined to attend, but De Molay with a retinue of Templars came to Paris as the Pope requested.

Philip IV was trying to weld France into an efficient kingdom, so it was inevitable that he should soon clash with the Templars. Secretly, Philip ordered the arrest of the Templars in France. Philip's *ballili* arrested every Templar whom they could apprehend during the early morning of October 13, 1307. The Templars were charged with heresy and other crimes against the Church. Those arrested were subjected to all the tortures devised by medieval jailers; this forced nearly all of them to confess to the crimes with

DEATH OF DE MOLAY AND DE CHARNEY
Grand Master Jacques De Molay and Grand Preceptor Guy De Charney
were burned at the stake on an island in the Seine, near Paris,
March 14, 1314.

which they were charged. Even De Molay and other high officers are said to have confessed.

De Molay Condemned

The proceedings against the Templars lasted five years before the Order was suppressed by the Papal Bull *In Excelso* on May 6, 1312. The Bull *Ad Providam,* May 2, 1312, transferred most of the properties of the Templars to the Knights of Saint John of the Hospital. Many of the Templars perished before the Order was suppressed. Among the survivors were Jacques de Molay, Grand Master, Guy de Charney, Grand Preceptor of Normandy, and other high officers of the Order. Philip determined to deal with the high officers as he chose. After several attempts to compel De Molay and De Charney to acknowledge their confessions publicly, Philip ordered them burned at the stake. On March 14, 1314, De Molay and De Charney were burned at the stake on an island in the Seine.

Many writers have attempted to prove or disprove the guilt or innocence of the Templars. Most writers maintain that the Templars were innocent of the crimes with which they were charged and were victims of the avaricious king who coveted their wealth. Some writers have contended that Philip's real motive was the preservation of his kingdom, but this seems to be an invention of Philip's apologists rather than a well-substantiated historical fact.

The Papal Bull *In Excelso,* suppressing the Order, was enforced in every country in Europe, but nowhere else was it enforced with the same brutality as in France. Even there some two or three thousand Templars escaped. Generally the Templars were allowed their freedom under a ban of excommunication. This prevented them as individuals or as an Order from entering any monastic or military orders until the ban was lifted.

Many theories have been advanced regarding the fate of the Templars who survived. Writers have developed interesting and romantic stories about their fate. One of these stories contends that the modern Masonic Templars are the lineal descendants of the soldier-friars, but this theory lacks at the moment conclusive historical evidence. On the other hand, it is conceivable that the philosophical ideals and ceremonials of the Order have been preserved by several organizations until they became a part of the modern Masonic system.

2. The Hospitallers

A hospital for Christian pilgrims, dedicated to Saint John, was founded in Jerusalem by a group of merchants from Amalfi in 1046. When the Crusaders stormed into Jerusalem on July 15, 1099, this small institution was sorely taxed to care for the wounded. As soon as order was restored in the conquered city, the Crusaders, under the leadership of Godfrey of Bouillon, bestowed many gifts on this institution. Crusading nobles returning to their homes in the west gave such glowing accounts of the services rendered by the Hospital of Saint John that many gifts were sent to it by nobles who had participated in the First Crusade.

Gerard, Master of the Hospital of Saint John, realized that, since the humble institution was becoming famous, it was necessary to place its affairs in order. Gerard and the few members of the brotherhood assumed the vows of chastity, obedience and poverty, and dedicated their lives to the service of the poor and the pilgrims who came to Jersusalem. The *Rule* adopted by the Order was similar to that of the Augustinian Canons. The Order's habit was a simple black robe with a white cross of eight points on the left side over the heart.

Pope Pascal II, in a Bull, February 15, 1113, placed the Order under his immediate protection. Due to the Pope's sanction and the wise leadership of Raymond du Puy, who became Grand Master on September 3, 1120, the possessions, membership, and services of the Order were greatly increased. Under Raymond du Puy, the Order assumed military duties similar to those performed by the Templars. Although the Order took an active part in the military affairs of the Latin Kingdom of Jerusalem, it remained primarily a nursing brotherhood.

When Acre fell in May, 1291, the Hospitallers, like the Templars, retired to the Island of Cyprus. During the first few years of its residence in Cyprus, the wealth and influence of the Order increased by additional gifts from the nobles in the west. In 1341, the estates of the Templars, which escaped seizures by secular rulers, were transferred by the Pope to the Hospitallers.

After the destruction of the Templars, the Hospitallers moved their headquarters to the Island of Rhodes. This island was strategically located as a center of commercial and military activities in the Eastern Mediterranean. When secular rulers failed to stamp out piracy, the Hospitallers assumed the duty, patrolling the lanes of sea travel. The naval services of the Order prevented the Saracens from using the sea as an avenue for large-scale conquest in Europe. During two centuries of operations from Rhodes, the Hospitallers never lost sight of their original purpose of constructing and maintaining hospitals for the poor.

In 1523, the Sultan Suleman captured Rhodes and the Hospitallers were forced to withdraw to Crete. In 1530, Charles V gave to the Order the Island of Malta. The Order now assumed the title by which it is best known— The Sovereign Order of the Knights of Malta. On Malta, the Order continued the naval war against the Saracens and pirates, serving also as a nursing brotherhood.

The Hospitallers in Malta

The Hospitallers' occupation of Malta came almost simultaneously with the Protestant Reformation. Most of the Order's possessions in England, Scotland, and Wales were seized by the Crown. The Order was able to retain some of its possessions in other lands, but gradually the remaining possessions were seized by secular rulers, and only Malta remained in the hands of the Order.

ISLAND OF MALTA, PORT OF VALLETTA

The Island of Malta, long the pass to the inner Mediterranean, was for centuries linked with the Order of St. John of Jerusalem or the Knights of Malta. The Port of Valletta was named for Grand Master La Vallette who, late in the 16th century, defeated a powerful Turkish fleet. King Charles of Spain granted Malta to the Knights in 1530.

On Malta the knights built a great fortification, Valletta, named for La Vallette, the hero of the siege of 1565. Valletta became the capital of the Order, which now assumed all the characteristics of a temporal power. Gradually the Order became less monastic and more aristocratic. Continuous naval warfare was waged against the Turks, who were now operating from their conquered territories in Southeastern Europe.

The supreme governing body of the Order was the Grand Chapter whose presiding officer was the Grand Master. Authority of the Grand Chapter was supreme and unalterable throughout the eight *langues* or territorial divisions of the Order. These eight divisions or *langues* were Provence, Auvergne, France, Aragon, England, Germany, Castille, and Portugal. A Chapter in each of the *langues* was held annually to administer the affairs of the territory under the edicts of the Grand Chapter and the Grand Master.

The membership of the Order was divided into three classes—knights, chaplains, and serving brothers. All wore black surplices upon which was emblazoned the eight-point Maltese Cross. Until the Order assumed the duty of policing the Mediterranean, only the knights were permitted to engage in battle. After the Order became a naval power, the serving brothers were divided into two subdivisions —servants-at-arms, who took their places in battle, and Brethren *de Stage,* who performed menial tasks.

Nearly all activities of the individual members and of the Order as a whole were controlled by a section in the *Rule* or constitution of the Order. All members were required to attend divine service and live as austerely as possible as men engaged in almost constant warfare. In striking contrast to other monastic orders, the *Rule* of the Hospitallers gave specific directions regarding cleanliness and toilet. No member could hold personal possessions. The *Rule* of the Order also contained adequate instructions for the care of the sick confined in the Order's hospitals and for the construction and maintenance of the hospital buildings.

The rise of nationalism throughout Europe had very little effect on the conduct and activities of the Order. The first political struggle in which the members were forced to take part was the French Revolution. The Order's sympathies were with the French Monarchy; consequently, when the monarchy fell, the estates of the Order were seized by the revolutionary government. In 1798, the French forces captured the Island of Malta. Under the terms of the Treaty of Paris in 1814, Malta was given to England.

After the loss of Malta, the Order was continued in Germany and Italy. The Italian branch embraced the Grand Priories of Rome, Venice, and Lombardy and Sicily; the German branch included the Grand Priory of Bohemia and several honorary organizations. There have been several attempts to enlarge the Order but none have been successful in restoring it to its former position of influence and power.

3. The Teutonic Knights

The Order of Teutonic Knights of Saint Mary's Hospital was founded in 1198. Its primary object was to care for Teutonic pilgrims who came to worship or fight in the wars

against the Saracens.   Unlike the Templars and Hospitallers, the Teutonic Knights achieved their greatest military
success not in the Holy Land but in Europe.   In 1229, the
Order began the conquest of Prussia.   When the Order
had completed this task, it surrendered its possessions to the
Pope and received them back as fiefs from the Holy See.

The Order defended its possessions against the Poles
and Russians for three centuries.   Immediately after each
conquest, the Order prepared for its defense by erecting
strong fortifications in the conquered territory.   The political changes in Europe did not affect the Order until the
Napoleonic Wars.   In 1801, all possessions west of the
Rhine were lost, and in 1809, the Order was suppressed
entirely and its possessions seized by the secular rulers.

CHAPTER IV

Theories Connecting Chivalric Freemasonry with the Medieval Order of Knights Templar

VARIOUS THEORIES have been proposed to prove the continued existence of the Order of Knights Templar after its suppression by the Papal Bull *In Excelso,* on May 6, 1314. Many able scholars have speculated on the fate of the individual Templars but none appear to have been able to accomplish the necessary research which would forever solve this perplexing historical problem. Most of the writers, who have worked on this problem, have either been very positive that the Masonic Order of Knights Templar has a direct connection with the medieval Order of Knights Templar or that there is no connection possible and that the Order perished completely in 1314 after the mandate of the Papal Bull had been carried out in all countries in Europe. Neither theory is entirely consistent with the facts as found in the existing material on this subject. The fault lies partly with the failure to cover the materials effectively and partly with a lack of full understanding of both Orders, i. e., the ancient and the modern Knights Templar.

Before offering the theories, which have been advanced tending to show a continuity in the existence of the Orders, it is well to call attention to certain established facts which will aid in the understanding of the problem.

It has been rather definitely determined that thousands of Templars escaped arrest and the fate which was that of those arrested. A group of Templars appeared before the Council of Vienne, convened to consider the fate of the Templars, in October, 1312, claiming to represent two thousand Templars who were hiding in the forests near Lyon, France. One writer has estimated that forty thousand members of the Order escaped arrest throughout France, and it seems that this figure is not unreasonable if it takes into account the sergeants, serving brothers, and chaplains as well as the knights. Only a small portion of the membership of the Order ever appeared before the Inquisition in Paris. The highest estimate placed on the arrests accomplished in France is 638 Templars, this figure being based on the number appearing before the various tribunals. One writer says that there were not fewer than 4,000 knights residing in France at the time of Philip's order of arrest. Outside of France the commands of the Papal Bull were carried out but authentic documents fail to account for all of the membership of the Order. It is definitely known that no other monarch enforced the Papal decree with the same severity as did Philip of France.

The Templars as Military Leaders

It is also well to consider the Templars as individuals before contemplating their fate after the suppression of the Order. The Templars were the finest professional soldiers of their day, perhaps among the finest the world has ever known. It does not seem possible that monarchs sorely pressed for trained soldiers would allow such a group to languish in a dungeon. What monarch would permit such a group of men to perish when there was need for them everywhere? Their arms were needed particularly in Spain, Hungary, Italy, and Portugal to drive back the advancing hordes of Islam. Even if every knight of the Order suffered arrest, this would not mean that the Order was entirely wiped out. For example, there were the sergeants, who, because of birth, were not permitted to become knights but who were well schooled in the art of warfare. Where did the sergeants go at the time of the suppression? Very likely into the organized armies of the great kings of the West, who did not regard a man's birth but only his ability to fight. Where, too, did the serving brothers go? This group included the finest artisans of the day, armourers, masons, carpenters, smiths, clerks, weavers and members of many

CHURCH OF THE HOLY SEPULCHRE, JERUSALEM

other trades. Quite naturally, when the Order was suppressed, the serving brothers went into the guilds of their trades where skilled men were sorely needed. It is possible that this group made a profound impression on the civilization of the time as they had seen the culture of the East and knew the fundamentals of the Eastern philosophies and arts.

Again, never in the history of the world has any ruler, no matter how powerful, been able to exterminate entirely a group as large as the Templars or to stamp out their cause. It seems absurd to think that a Papal Bull, even in the fourteenth century, could effect the mass execution of 50,000 members of such an Order as were the Knights Templar. Historical evidence does not bear out the fact of this mass execution, consequently all theories holding the continuance of the Order into more recent times would seem to have a reasonable basis of fact.

In addition, we find that Chivalric Freemasonry offers considerable internal evidence to show an organic connecting link between the two Orders. Internal evidence tending to show this connection includes the following:

1. Name.
2. Ritualistic ceremonials.
3. Beauseant.
4. The battle cry of the Ancient Templars:
   "Non nobis, Domine, non nobis sed nomini tuo da gloriam."
5. Symbolism of the medieval Orders as exemplified in the modern Templars.

While it is possible that these internal evidences could have been carried over bodily by some ritualist, it seems highly improbable that so many of them would have been present in Chivalric Freemasonry at its very first appearance. It seems much more likely that some of these had existed in the secret traditions of Freemasonry and became more and more evident as the ethical system of Freemasonry developed over the centuries.

The allegorical illustrations used by the medieval Order of Knights Templar were possibly used by several organizations before they became distinctively the property of Chivalric Freemasonry. It is a well accepted fact, that philosophical and esoteric organizations change form frequently and that, upon dissolution, their practices are taken up often by other organizations. Philosophers and students have pointed out the continuance of many different ideas, which were apparently dead but which suddenly and without apparent cause have been revived when a new necessity for them arose. Is it not possible that the secret traditions of the Templars survived in like manner and are now an essential part of what we call Chivalric Freemasonry?

Six Important Theories

Historians have offered the following theories in support of the notion of an organic connection between the ancient and the modern Knights Templar:

1. That secret priories continued in England (also possibly, elsewhere) after the suppression.
2. That the Templars entered the masons' guilds and preserved their ritual in these groups.
3. That the Templars who entered the Order of Christ preserved their ritual, and subsequently permitted it to become a part of Freemasonry.
4. That fugitive Templars under John Marc Larmenius organized a Grand Priory and eventually became the *Ordre du Temple* in France.
5. That fugitive Templars fled to Sweden and under Pierre d'Aumont organized a Grand Priory and were absorbed eventually by Freemasonry as the "Rite of Strict Observance."
6. That the Templars, who entered the Order of St. John of the Hospital in Scotland, dominated that Order and, at the time of the Reformation, joined the Freemasons.

CHAPTER V

THEORIES OF MASONIC TEMPLAR ORIGINS

EACH OF THE theories mentioned in the preceding chapter has its advocates, who have published many books and articles to support their contentions. It is impossible to give a full review of each of these theories here but some of the more pertinent facts as to each theory are presented below.

1. *Secret Priories in England*

This theory was first advanced, it seems, to support the claim of the old Encampment of Baldwyn as the ranking encampment in England. It is not unlikely that secret priories came into existence in various places after the suppression of the Order in 1314. It has always been a part of the aftermath of every great war or other movement for the participants to organize into more or less formal groups to keep alive old friendships and to perpetuate the memories of the conflict. The Templars were veterans of many wars, so it is not impossible that, after the Order was suppressed, they united, in many communities, to keep alive their close associations born on the field of battle. If the Templars did unite into such formal groups they naturally assumed the same character as that under which they had fought. Because of Papal Bulls, these would have had to be secret societies. If such societies of Templars were formed throughout Europe, and in England particularly, it is not surprising that at least one of them survived. The old Encampment at Baldwyn may have been just such a one to survive the four centuries between the suppression of the old order and the first public notice of Chivalric Freemasonry.

This theory has not been advanced as frequently as some others but it is not on that account less plausible. Since it has not received the attention it seems to merit, authentic

MIDDLE TEMPLE LIBRARY (London)

The English Knights Templar had quite extensive property holdings in the early 14th century. Among these were the Inner and Middle Temple Buildings. Today these same buildings constitute with two other groups what is known as the Inns of Court, and are actually a vast Law School. Above:—Middle Temple Library from a print by Tony Grubhofer.

documentary evidence in support of it is lacking at the moment. In order to test this theory it will be necessary to examine the existing records in England for proof of an extant organization which would correspond to the En-campment of Baldwyn. This will require the examination of not only the royal charters and laws but of certain borough and church records as well. It may be discovered eventually that this is one of the connecting links between the two organizations.

2. *The Templars and the Masons' Guilds*

Many writers have contended that this theory was first advanced by Andrew Michael Ramsey, an adherent of the Stuart cause in Scotland. Several versions of his speech on the subject have been printed and the best authorities quote the following extract from this speech:

> At the time of the Crusades in Palestine many princes, lords and citizens associated themselves and vowed to re-store the Temple of the Christians in the Holy Land, to employ themselves in bringing back their architecture to its first institution. They agreed upon several ancient signs and symbolic words drawn from the well of religion in order to recognize themselves amongst the heathen and Saracens. These signs and words were only communicated to those who promised solemnly, even sometimes at the foot of the altar, never to reveal them. This sacred promise was, therefore, not an execrable oath, as it has been called, but a respectable bond to unite Christians of all nationalities in one confraternity. Some time afterwards our Order formed an intimate union with the Knights of St. John of Jerusalem. From that time our Lodges took the name of this union, which was made after the example set by the Israelites when they erected the second Temple who, whilst they handled the trowel and mortar with one, in the other held the sword and buckler.

In spite of the lavish claims made by the Chevalier Ramsey and those who use his speech as a means to connect the two Orders, it seems that the speech lacked not only direct information on the case but also that Ramsey was himself drawing too heavily on the degree of Scotch Master, which was a part of the system of Freemasonry in France at that time. Dr. Oliver quotes two authorities who affirmed the belief that the Templars and Freemasonry had been in close relationship for a long period. The first of these was an opponent of Freemasonry, from whom Dr. Oliver quotes:

Barruel, however, expressly asserts that the whole system of Masonry was derived from the Templars. 'The whole of your school, and all your Lodges,' says he, 'descend from the Templars.' After the extinction of their Order, a certain number of criminal knights, who had escaped the general proscription, formed a body to perpetuate their frightful mysteries. They formed adepts who were to perpetuate and transmit from generation to generation the same mysteries of initiation, the same oaths, etc. These mysteries have descended to you (Freemasons) and you perpetuate their impiety, their oaths, and hatred. Such is your origin. Length of time, the manners of each age, may have varied some of your signs, and of your shocking systems; but the essence is the same, and the plots are similar. You would not think it, but everything betrayed your forefathers, and everything betrays their progeny. (History of Jacobinism, vol. II, p. 378.)

Dr. Oliver also quotes another authority on the same theory:

A talented living Brother is persuaded that the Templars' Order has been preserved in the system of Freemasonry from the period of its proscription. These are his words: 'I am fully convinced that the Order of the Templars was received by them (the Masons), and to our days preserved, with its constitution, ceremonials, and titles, as a Christian Order. This is well attested by the Grand Lodge of Kilwinning, and several conclaves established in Scotland, England, Ireland, and particularly in France.' (Husenbeth's Essay, in the Freemasons' Quarterly Review, 1838, p. 29.)

Dr. Oliver concludes his evaluation of this theory by quoting from an eminent Masonic historian, as follows:

A singular coincidence is recorded by Clavel (p. 355), which appears to give color to the hypothesis which assimilates Templarism with Freemasonry. He says that, in the seventeenth century, there was discovered in Germany, within the grave of a Templar, who died before the dissolution of the Order, a stone inscribed with sundry diagrams connected with Freemasonry, viz., the square and compasses; the pentalpha; the celestial sphere; a star of five points and several other stars. The Masonic emblem is also found on Templar monuments.

A Source of Grave Error

It would appear that each of these authorities has drawn on the sources more heavily than the sources deserve and that they make the same error that is so frequently made in connecting the two Orders. The most frequently appearing error is that authorities try to connect the two orders by drawing on the chivalry of the knights and, at the same time, entirely overlooking the other members of the medieval order.

Claud Keltner, an American student of the subject, has advanced the theory that the most probable connecting link exists in ritualistic observances of the masons' guilds, which were introduced by the serving brothers of the Order of the Temple, who had joined the guilds after the suppression of the Templars. While the old manuscript constitutions of the masons' guilds in England do not mention any strictly Christian observances, it is definitely known that the French operative craftsmen had far more elaborate ceremonials than did their English brethren and that portions of them were entirely Christian, patterned after the vows of the Templars. This was notably true after the French craftsmen took to the road and became organized as a traveling society of masons closely allied with other trades and the monastic brotherhoods. The French travelling masons assumed more closely the form of a monastic fraternity than did the craftsmen in any other country. Keltner assumes that the serving brothers had knowledge of at least a portion of the ritualistic ob-

TEMPLE CHURCH (London)

When the English Order of Knights Templar was dissolved in 1314, their great holdings became the property of the crown. They later came into the possession of the Knights of St. John, who in 1346 leased them to students of common law. Above:—The "Round" of the Temple Church in which the nine stone Knights Templar are seen. The prone figures are within the two iron rail enclosures.

servances of the Order of Knights Templar. He believes that, due to their superiority in workmanship, education, and experience, they dominated the various guilds and were able to dominate completely the existing masons' companies after the suppression of the Templars. While this theory seems rather plausible, it, too, lacks at present full documentary evidence to prove its point.

3. *The Templars and the Order of Christ*

It is a well established fact that the King of Portugal, Dion II, refused to suppress the Templars entirely. Instead, he created a new order called the Order of Christ. Many writers have thought that this Order was a continuation of the old Order of Templars and that it furnishes the connecting link between the medieval order of Knights Templar and Chivalric Freemasonry. We can offer no better description of the Order of Christ in this connection than to quote portions of an article by H. C. de Lafontaine in *Ars Quatuor Coronatorum,* and some of the comment thereon.

[John Yarker in Vol. II.] Although the Order of Knights Templar was suppressed by the martyrdom of its Grand Master in 1314, it has never been entirely extinguished . . . The King of Portugal protected the Order in his dominions, but acceded to the request of Pope John XXII, in 1319, to change the name to 'Knights of Christ' and change the red cross of the order with a white one. With these slight changes the Order remained intact until 1522, when the then Portuguese King made the Crown its Master.

[Ladislas de Malczovitch in Vol. XVII.] That the Order of Christ is in some sense, at least, a continuation of the Templars, is well known.

[W. J. Castle in Vol. XX] It is known that in Spain the Templars were fully acquitted, and, though when Clement suppressed the Order, the Templars ceased to exist as such, the brethren and their property were only transferred to another Order.

[Chetwode Crawley in Vol. XXVI.] Now and again it has been assumed that the Order of Christ perpetuated in some way the Order of the Temple. It was asserted that the intimate relations existing in the first half of the nineteenth century between the Freemasonry of Ireland and the Freemasonry of Portugal might well be the channel through which the Templar traditions reached modern Freemasonry. Beyond similarity of object, however, no connection can be discerned between the two Orders.

... As Knights Templar they were pledged to hold aloft what was to them the symbol of salvation, but evil communications often corrupt good manners, and the glamour and softness of the East dimmed in many cases the most pious resolutions. In process of time they accumulated riches, they heaped up riches to their own destruction, and the downfall came, swift as vengeance from on high, to remind them of their tarnished faith. But were they as guilty as they were to a large extent the victims of the cupidity of a French king and the insensate envy of an unrelenting Pope? And the end of it was, that both these personages perished miserably soon after their insatiate thirst for wealth and property had been satisfied. Portugal was the happy exception to the universal scene of carnage, and I do believe that this little country preserved to us the Templar traditions through a considerable period, almost till our modern system of Templary came into existence ... It was only through the incompetence of subsequent rulers, whose riotous extravagance sapped the life-blood of the nation, that she fell into the decadent position in which she now is, a country almost without a remnant of her former greatness, and yet in all these varying changes the constant and firm ally of the English nation.

... Suffice it to say that to conciliate all things, King Deniz, or Denis, the wise and beneficent ruler of Portugal at that time, conceived a means by which all contentions might be put to rest, and that was to convert the Templars into a new Order, and to restore Templarism in Portugal in a new form. He submitted the idea to the Pope, who approved of it, and on March 15th, 1319, John XXII, the reigning Pontiff, published a Bull creating a new military Order in Portugal, under the name, style, and title of the *Order of Christ*. This new Order held somewhat similar rules to those of the Templars. The Pope appointed as Grand Master of the new Order a Knight of the Order of Aviz, and the former Master of the Templars, Vassco Fernandes, entered the order as a simple knight. King Denis, in bestowing the properties of the Templars on the Order, expressly stated that 'the Order of Christ was created in reformation of the Order of the Temple, which had been dissolved.'

. . . He also gave the new Order the castle of Castro-Marim, and here the *Cross of Christ* brethren established themselves. All former Templars resident in Portugal entered the new Order as professed knights; only one individual was foreign to the old Order, and that was the new Grand Master, Gil Martin, who, as we have already heard, belonged to the Order of Aviz . . .

. . . the investiture of the Master. This took place in the chapel of the royal palace. King Denis was present, with the members of his Court, also the following ecclesiastics: the Bishops of Evora, Guarda, Viseu, and Lamogo. All the knights of the Order of Aviz accompanied the Master Elect, who had governed them for three years, being a model of prudence and wisdom and whom they were yielding up to the new Order. After the usual religious ceremony, celebrated with great pomp, the prelate of Cister (or Cintra) removed the habit of the former Order, and invested the Master of the new Order with the white scapula and cap belonging to it, and delivered up to him the sword, seal, and flag, with the Cross of Christ quarted thereon in red and white.

When the first Master died in 1321, . . .

. . . He [Prince Henry, the navigator, the third son of John I.] claims our attention as having been in due course Master of the Order of Christ. He reformed the statutes of the Order, and for that purpose held a general chapter in 1449. He also made Thomar the capitular place of assembly . . .

King Manuel, who succeeded Prince Henry in the Mastership of the Order of Christ, who was noted for his interest in all that pertained to architecture, and whose memory is perpetuated by that peculiar style of ornamentation known as Manueline, set about enlarging the church at Thomar. A new impetus was given later to building operations by King John III, who converted the Order into a monastic brotherhood, making constructing of living-quarters a necessity. The master of the works was the great Portuguese architect, João de Castilho, who added a nave to the church, and built four of the five dormitories of the West cloisters; the main cloister, begun in 1545 by João, was finished by another prominent architect, Diego de Terralva, in 1562. In 1580 Phillip II, King of Portugal, was crowned before the church door, and the importance of Thomar was at an end.

Comments on the Order of Christ

Comments by Members on the Article by H. D. de Lafontaine, "The Portuguese Order of Christ"

B. Telepneff writes:

. . . In France and England, suppression instead of substitution would favor a secret tradition. Although the charter of Larmenius has been condemned as a forgery, this was chiefly because the transcript failed to abbreviate words in the manner of a document of the time of Larmenius. But when the original Charter in cypher was brought to light, the abbreviations were found to be there. The document is not as old as the time of Larmenius, but this can be explained if the custodians replaced a wornout manuscript with a true copy and destroyed the original in the interests of secrecy. Of course, it can be explained, like all old manuscripts, as the product of an anonymous forger at an unknown date in an unknown place. The value of this explanation is that any indications of genuineness can be attributed to the skill of the supposed forger.

Bro. Malczovitch when taking the English Masonic degree of Knight Templar recognized one of the signs as being given traditionally by the Ghost of a Templar suicide in Hungary. Coincidence cannot be ruled out, but seems rather far-fetched. My own belief is that, until comparatively recent times, tradition, going back in some cases to the stone age, formed a great part of the knowledge of the mass of people. Within the fellowships, gossip relating to other and defunct fellowships must have been transmitted as pearls of wisdom to be expanded into revivals of fellowships when the need or opportunity arose.

There seem to be many points in favor of this theory which are worthy of consideration. As shown by the article quoted, the Order of Christ took an active interest in the construction of many buildings and the members were consequently thrown into close contact with the operative craftsmen. It is not impossible that these masons' companies adopted some of the ceremonials of the Order of Christ because all except those of the reception of candidates were open to the public in one or another of the chapels of the Order. Another point in favor of this theory is that Philip, Duke of Orleans, sent two Frenchmen to Lisbon to obtain the secret ceremonials of this Order when Philip was instituting the *Ordre du Temple* in France in 1705. Although the two representatives of Philip were arrested by the Portuguese authorities and consequently did not obtain the ceremonials as planned, this incident does show that there was a well established belief that the Order of Christ was the legal and organic successor of the Templars.

One point here, which has never been fully explored by scholars, is the possible connection between the Order of Christ and the Irish Freemasons in the seventeenth century. The advocates of Irish liberty were avowed admirers of the Portuguese and the people of the two countries were very friendly during the closing decades of that century. Since the majority of the Freemasons in Portugal were Catholic, it seems natural that they would be on better terms with the Irish Freemasons, who were also Catholic, than with the English who were mostly Protestant. This seems likely also for the reason that many of the earliest evidences of Chivalric Freemasonry are to be found in France and some writers believe that Masonic Order of the Temple was first worked in that country.

4. *"Ordre du Temple" in France*

The theory that this Order is the "connecting link" between the ancient and the modern Templars, is supported by a supposed Charter of Transmission whereby Jacques De Molay was supposed to have transmitted the Grand Mastership of the Order of Knights Templar through successive Grand Masters down to John Marc Larmenius. One copy of this famous document still exists and portions of it have been reprinted in *Ars Quatuor Coronatorum*. The existing copy is written in a code not unfamiliar to members of York Rite Freemasonry. Before commenting on the authenticity of the document it seems not unwise to quote a translation:

I, Brother John Marc Larmenius, of Jerusalem, by the grace of God and the secret decree of the most venerable and holy martyr, the Grand Master of the Soldiery of the Temple (to whom be honor and glory), confirmed by the common council of the brethren, being endowed with the Supreme Grand Mastership of the whole Order of the Temple, to every one who shall see these letters decretal thrice greeting:

Be it known to all, both present and to come, that the failure of my strength, on account of extreme age, my poverty, and the weight of government being well considered, I, the aforesaid humble Master of the Soldiery of the Temple, have determined, for the greater glory of God and the protection and safety of the Order, the brethren, and the statutes, to resign the Grand Mastership into stronger hands.

On which account, God helping, and with the consent of a Supreme Convention of Knights, I have conferred, and by this present decree do confer, for life, the authority and prerogatives of Grand Master of the Order of the Temple upon the Eminent Commander and very dear brother, Francis Thomas Theobald Alexandrinus, with the power, according to time and circumstances, of conferring the Grand Mastership of the Order of the Temple and the supreme authority upon another brother, most eminent for the nobility of his education and talent and decorum of his manners: which is done for the purpose of maintaining a perpetual succession of Grand Masters, an uninterrupted series of successors, and the integrity of the statutes. Nevertheless, I command that the Grand Mastership shall not be transmitted without the consent of a general convention of the fellow-soldiers of the Temple, as often as that Supreme Convention desires to be convened; and, matters being thus conducted, the successor shall be elected at the pleasure of the knights.

But, lest the powers of the supreme office should fall

into decay, now and forever let there be four Vicars of the Grand Master, possessing supreme power, eminence and authority over the whole Order, with the reservation of the rights of the Grand Master; which Vicars of the Grand Master shall be chosen from among the elders, according to the order of their profession.   Which is decreed in accordance with the above-mentioned wish, commended to me and to the brethren by our most venerable and most blessed Master, the martyr, to whom be honor and glory.   Amen.

Finally, in consequence of a decree of a Supreme Convention of the brethren, and by the supreme authority to me committed, I will, declare, and command that the Scottish Templars, as deserters from the Order, are to be accursed, and that they and the brethren of St. John of Jerusalem (upon whom may God have mercy), as spoliators of the domains of our soldiery, are now and hereafter to be considered as beyond the pale of the Temple.

I have therefore established signs, unknown to our false brethren, and not to be known by them, to be orally communicated to our fellow-soldiers, and in which way I have already been pleased to communicate them in the Supreme Convention.

But these signs are only to be made known after due profession and knightly consecration, according to the statutes, rites, and usages of the fellow-soldiery of the Temple, transmitted by me to the above named Eminent Commander as they were delivered into my hands by the venerable and most holy martyr, our Grand Master, to whom be honor and glory.   Let it be done as I have said.   So mote it be.   Amen.

I, Francis Thomas Theobaldus Alexandrinus, God helping, have accepted the Grand Mastership, 1324.

For the sake of brevity we have not quoted the long list of Grand Masters whose signatures are supposed to appear after that of Francis Thomas Theobaldus Alexandrinus. The last signature is that of Bernard Raymund Fabré, who is well known to Masonic scholars.   His date is 1804.

Opinions of Historians on the "Charter of Transmission"

Albert G. Mackey assumes the document was a forgery, but offers the following comment:

In 1705, Philip of Orleans, who was subsequently the regent of France during the minority of Louis XV, collected together the remnants of this society, which still secretly existed, but had changed its object from a licentious to one of a political character. He caused new statutes to be constructed; and an Italian Jesuit, by name Father Bonani, who was a learned antiquary and an excellent designer, fabricated the document now known as the Charter of Larmenius, and thus pretended to attach the new society to the ancient Order of the Templars.

As this chapter is not the least interesting of those forged documents with which the history of Freemasonry unfortunately abounds, a full description of it here will not be out of place.

The theory of the Duke of Orleans and his accomplice Bonani was (and the theory is still maintained by the Order of the Temple at Paris); that when James de Molay was about to suffer at the stake, he sent for Larmenius, and in prison, with the consent and approbation of such of his knights as were present, appointed him his successor, with the right of making a similar appointment before his death. On the demise of Molay, Larmenius accordingly assumed the office of Grand Master, and ten years after issued this charter, transmitting his authority to Theobaldus Alexandrinus, by whom it was in like manner transmitted through a long line of Grand Masters, until in 1705 it reached Philip, Duke of Orleans. It will be seen hereafter that the list was subsequently continued to a later period.

Several other writers have contended that this famous document was a forgery and was the work of Father Bonani, or that of some other clever forger, possibly even Bernard Raymond Fabré. Findel declares that the document was a counterfeit because:

. . . (1) The Latin is not that of the 14th century. (2) The ancient Templar statutes are ignorantly and superficially treated, as no Grand Master was permitted to elect a successor . . . (3) This deed was quite unnecessary for the preservation of the Grand Mastership, for if a convention existed, it elected without charter, and if no convention existed, then would the charter be of no avail. (4) The installation of four general vicars was the more unnecessary now,

as at the period when the order was at its height they had
not needed them, the Grand Master having required but
two assistants . . . (5) If the *Scoti Templarii* mentioned in
the Charta meant the Freemason degrees, and these at
length renounced Jesuitism and political intrigue, and the
Parisian Templars on the other hand struck out a non-
Masonic path for themselves, while the Masonic Convention
in Wiesbaden in 1782 excluded the Templars from Masonic
lodges, then can the Anathema in the Charta against the
Scottish degrees only have been pronounced at that date,
consequently the document must then have been drawn up . . .

Frederick J. W. Crowe, the owner of a copy of the Charter
of Transmission, replies:

. . . To these objections I would reply: (1) The Latin
is quite consistent with a fourteenth century origin, as will
be seen on reference to my copy. [The Latin text quoted by
Crowe differs from that given by Thory in *Acta Latomorum*
which was used by Findel.] (2) Larmenius states, 'Therefore with the help of God, and with sole consent of the
Supreme Assembly of Knights, I have conferred,' etc. (3
and 4). The confusion of the Order, what remnants of it
were left, might well account for new methods of procedure.
(5) What proof does Findel bring of his assertion that 'this
deed was without any doubt prepared under rule of his
predecessor, Cosse Brissac (1776-1792)'? . . .

. . . The Charter has been carefully examined for me by
Sir George Warner, Keeper of the Manuscripts of the British Museum, who is one of the greatest experts on the subject. He says, that, whilst the Latin is that of the fourteenth century, the illumination cannot be, but it may be any
time from the latter part of the fifteenth century, so that
we seem no nearer to the true history of this remarkable
document than before.

It seems that Mr. Crowe has correctly stated the case in his
closing remark and that the document still lacks confirming
evidence on either side of the controversy. Although the
claims advanced by those, who contend that the document
is genuine, are of long standing, it seems that little or no
effort has been made to locate other copies of the Charter
of Transmission or to try to trace the long list of Grand

GÉNÉALOGIE DE LA FRANC-MAÇONNERIE TEMPLIÈRE.

(Les lignes pointillées indiquent les liaisons hypothétiques ou légendaires.)

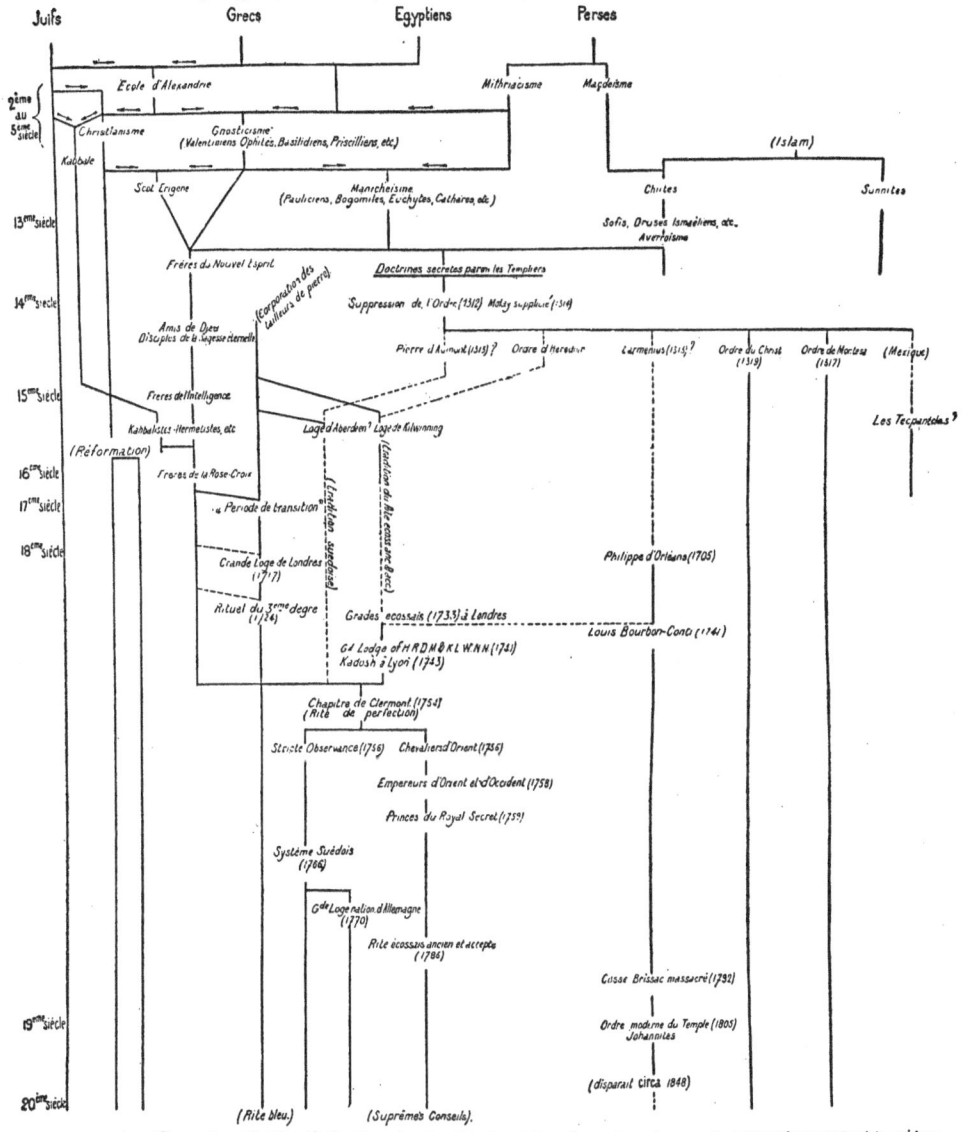

Juifs   Grecs   Egyptiens   Perses

2ème au 5ème siècle

École d'Alexandrie   Mithriacisme   Magdéisme

Christianisme

Gnosticisme (Valentiniens Ophites, Basilidiens, Priscilliens, etc.)   (Islam)

Kabbale

Scot Érigène   Manichéisme (Pauliciens, Bogomiles, Euchytes, Cathares, etc.)   Chiites   Sunnites

13ème siècle   Sofis, Druses Ismaéliens, etc. Averroïsme

Frères du Nouvel Esprit   Doctrines secrètes parmi les Templiers

14ème siècle   (Corporation des tailleurs de pierre)   Suppression de l'Ordre (1312) Molay supplicié (1314)

Amis de Dieu Disciples de la Sagesse éternelle   Pierre d'Aumont (1313)?   Ordre d'Hérédom   Larmenius (1313)?   Ordre du Christ (1319)   Ordre de Montesa (1317)   (Mexique)

15ème siècle   Frères de l'Intelligence   Les Tecpantlas?

Kabbalistes-Hermétistes, etc.   Loge d'Aberdeen? Loge de Kilwinning

(Réformation)

16ème siècle   Frères de la Rose-Croix   (L'initiation supérieure)   (Corhèsion du Rite écossais avec d'autres)

17ème siècle

18ème siècle   "Période de transition"   Philippe d'Orléans (1705)

Grande Loge de Londres (1717)

Rituel du 3ème degré (1724)   Grades écossais (1733) à Londres   Louis Bourbon-Conti (1741)

Gd Lodge of HRDMØKLWNN (1741)
Kadosh à Lyon (1743)

Chapitre de Clermont (1754) (Rite de perfection)

Stricte Observance (1756)   Chevaliers d'Orient (1756)

Empereurs d'Orient et d'Occident (1758)

Princes du Royal Secret (1759)

Système Suédois (1766)

Gde Loge nation. d'Allemagne (1770)

Rite écossais ancien et accepté (1786)

Cossac Brissac massacré (1792)

19ème siècle   Ordre moderne du Temple (1805) Johannites

(disparaît circa 1848)

20ème siècle   (Rite bleu.)   (Suprêmes Conseils).

Les chiffres entre parenthèse n'impliquent pas nécessairement la date de la constitution des grades, mais celle de la première constatation de leur existence.

TEMPLAR GENEALOGY

This elaborate chart of the Knights Templar was prepared by an advocate of French Templary. He calls it "Genealogy of Templar Freemasonry," and, while it contains some inconsistencies, it throws some interesting sidelights on the subject.

Masters set forth in it. Until these things have been accomplished no definite conclusions can be drawn from this theory.

One of the advocates of French Templary has prepared an elaborate chart which is supposed to trace the origin of the Masonic Knights Templar and which he calls: "Genealogy of Templar Freemasonry." While it must be admitted, that the chart contains many inconsistencies, it throws some interesting sidelights on this phase of our subject.

5. *Fugitive Templars under Pierre d'Aumont*

One of the persistent theories of the continuance of the Order of Knights Templar is the theory suggested by the so-called "Rite of Strict Observance." It has been claimed that many of the Templars fled from France after the suppression and joined other Templars in Sweden under the leadership of Pierre d'Aumont, a preceptor of the Order. D'Aumont reorganized the fugitives into an effective combat unit and aided the Teutonic Knights in the subjugation of the region around the Baltic Sea.

One account of d'Aumont's activity holds that he fled first to Scotland, where he and his companions joined the forces of Robert Bruce and fought at Bannockburn. After the constitution of a new order of knighthood by Robert Bruce, the Templars, unwilling to surrender their identity, are said to have removed their operations to Sweden.

This theory of the continuance of the Order of Knights Templar was first introduced by the adherents of Baron Von Hund in the establishment of the "Rite of Strict Observance." Although not definitely established, the best authorities agree, that Von Hund received his Templar Order in Clermont, France, in 1740. If this is true, it would seem that the ritual used was based on one of the so-called "degrees of vengeance," as one was being worked in Clermont at that time. This degree was based on the martyrdom of Jacques de Molay and the subsequent fate of both

Philip IV of France and Clement V, the Pope. If this was the case, it appears that it was natural for the adherents of Von Hund to look for a connecting link between the medieval order of Knights Templar and the "Rite of Strict Observance."

The adherents of this theory publish a list of Grand Masters, which is as complete as that published by those supporting the continuance of the order under John Marc Larmenius. These writers do not offer the necessary supporting documents but contend that the names on their list are sufficiently well substantiated. No claim to legal authority, such as is supposed to be contained in the "Charter of Transmission," is offered by those supporting d'Aumont as the successor of de Molay.

This theory, although one of the first offered, has never been fully investigated. In its favor are many accounts of Templars fighting in the forces of the Teutonic Knights and rulers of the small kingdoms around the Baltic in the fourteenth century. Also worthy of note is the contention that d'Aumont was at Clermont when the Order was suppressed because the fugitive Templars rallied at that point to secure a hearing before the Pope in 1314.

All in all, this theory should have serious consideration in any investigation seeking to establish the connecting link between the two Orders.

6. *The Templars in Scotland*

There have been some writers who advocated the idea that the Templars continued their existence in Scotland, both as an independent organization and as a part of the Order of St. John of the Hospital. More has been written on this theory than on any other but it nevertheless still lacks conclusive proof. Dr. Oliver says:

During the fourteenth century, the Templars had come to honorable terms with the Hospitallers, and lived together in the same preceptories. Various royal charters mention this fact, and speak of the two Orders in distinct terms. Private charters of the fifteenth and sixteenth centuries mention the Templars and the Templar lands, without any allusion to the Hospitallers; so that, although the two bodies lived together, some at least of their lands were not in common . . .

Dr. Oliver to prove his contention then continues:

About the year 1560, the Preceptor of the Hospitallers, with several knights, who, like himself, had become Presbyterians, assisted by some esquires and serving brethren, met and formed a Chapter at Stirling. They assembled for initiation in the adjoining abbey of Cambus Kenneth, and subsequently connected themselves with a Lodge of Freemasons at Stirling, which was patronized by King James. It is probable that the whole of the knights had become Masons, but there appears to be some doubt whether they practiced the symbolical Masonry of the present day. And it is also a question which does not admit of a demonstrative solution, whether the Templars of the Crusades were Brothers of the Masonic Order. Nor can I learn when the Stirling Templars laid down the sword, and put on aprons. It is clear, however, that they were commonly known by the name of "Cross-legged Masons"; but this might be because they were a secret society, and members of the Stirling Lodge . . .

Freemasonry flourished during the reign of Charles II, and many new lodges were constituted in England . . . and many new degrees were invented and practiced in the continental Lodges, although they were not numerous at that period. These lodges became the rendezvous of the partisans of James, and by their means they held communication with their friends in England, thus giving political character to the new degrees, which those of simple Masonry would not bear.

Between the two unsuccessful attempts to establish the claim of the Stuarts to the throne of Great Britain, an enthusiastic admirer of that unfortunate family made his appearance on the Masonic stage. He was learned, pious, and polite; and as Freemasonry had been used as a tie to cement the adherents of James more closely, so the Chevalier Ramsay made use of the same machinery to extend the interests of the Pretender. And for the purpose of excluding all existing Masons who were not prepared for partisanship, he invented three new degrees, which he called Ecossais, Novice, and Knight Templar, affirming that they date their origin from the crusades, and that Godfrey de Bouillon was the Grand Master. These new degrees gave the impulse to the establishment of the *hauts grades,* which a French writer very properly denominàtes "superfetations."

RUINS OF MELROSE ABBEY

The Chancel, Melrose Abbey, Scotland, where under the High Altar before the large window shown, the heart of Robert the Bruce was deposited. D'Aumont and a number of fugitive Templars fled to Scotland and joined the cause of King Robert.

John Yarker, who spent much time in research on the theories of Chivalric Freemasonry, supports Dr. Oliver's statements in the following:

In Scotland the name Knights Templar is frequently found in documents from 1314 to 1590, though there was clearly a nominal united order, as James IV, in 1488, confirmed by Patent the property granted by his predecessor to the *'Sancti Hospitali de Jerusalem et fratribus eiusdem Militiae Templi Salomonis"* . . .

Yarker was convinced of the connection between the two orders and this theory of organic succession through Scotland deserves a very careful and detailed investigation.

The Templars and the Knights of Malta

In addition to the above lines of suggested investigation,

one other lead, which must not be overlooked, is the influence which the Templars could have exerted upon the Knights of St. John of the Hospital and which would have been most important after the knights took up their residence at Malta. Some have contended that the Knights of St. John did not admit the fugitive Templars to the Order, supporting their contention by pointing out the enmity which had existed between the two Orders during their sojourn in the Holy Land.

This contention not only lacks historical proof but also the elements of logical investigation. The Knights of St. John of the Hospital were as severely depleted in ranks after the retreat from Acre in 1291 as were the Templars. After the retreat both orders took up temporary quarters at Cyprus which was owned by the Templars. The Knights of St. John captured the Island of Rhodes on August 5, 1310, and established their headquarters there. It does not seem possible that the Knights of St. John would refuse membership in their Order to the Templars as individuals when they were anxious not only to hold Rhodes but also to rebuild their Order. Some have contended that the papal decree of excommunication would have prevented the Knights of St. John from admitting the Templars but it must be remembered that many Templars were freed of this ban and, as individuals, could have joined the Knights of St. John.

One of the points in favor of this theory is, that it is definitely known that many of the Knights of St. John were Freemasons during the early decades of the eighteenth century. Thory says in this connection:

The Inquisition persecuted the Freemasons at Malta. The Grand Master proscribed the assemblies of Freemasons under severe penalties, and six of the knights were sent into perpetual exile for having attended a lodge.

If the Templars, who joined the Knights of St. John, were able to exert a pronounced influence on the members of this Order, it may be that this is the connecting link between the two Orders. If, as some contend, the Templars had a secret ritual, is it not possible that that ritual was continued after the Templars joined the Knights of St. John but not given to any except to a limited few and then only after they had been sworn to secrecy; and that it was finally brought into the Masonic system by the Knights expelled, as Thory says, in 1741? Certainly this offers a worthwhile suggestion for further consideration and study.

CHAPTER VI

TEMPLAR RITUALS

THE STUDY of Templar rituals, from the viewpoint of one interested in the development of the rituals of the Grand Encampment of the United States, resolves itself into a study of three grades, namely, the Order of the Red Cross, the Order of Malta, and the Order of the Temple. Each of these grades may, in general, be subdivided into the story within the United States and the story in foreign countries.

During the past several years a decided beginning has been made by the Grand Encampment's Committee on Templar History in the task of studying the origin and development of Templar rituals. The work so far has been mainly the collection of source material, such as copies of old rituals and rituals of other jurisdictions as well as reports of various committees of the Grand Encampment and the several Grand Commanderies together with the listing of all rituals referred to in the literature of Masonry which might have bearing upon the subject.

Order of the Red Cross

In the study of the Order of the Red Cross several old rituals, some dating back as early as 1800-1815, have been located. In connection with this Order, considerable attention has been given to the companion degrees of the Scottish Rite, namely, *Knight of the East or Sword* and *Prince of Jerusalem*. Some very interesting leads regarding the reasons for the similarity of the rituals of these degrees have been uncovered. These leads will require considerable additional research work to investigate completely.

Order of Malta

Of the three Orders, the Order of Malta has had the least amount of work done on it so far as a study of its ritual is concerned.   Rituals in use by the several Great Priories in various parts of the world have been collected. Some older versions of these rituals have also been obtained.

Order of the Temple

The ritual of the Order of the Temple has so far presented the most satisfactory research results as well as a number of very interesting and, as yet, unsolved problems.

First, let us consider the rituals in use in the United States. The first national ritual was adopted at the triennial conclave of the Grand Encampment held at St. Louis in 1886. This ritual has been changed in part since that time but is today essentially the same as that adopted in 1886. Prior to this date the various Grand Commanderies had their own particular versions. The outstanding ones seem to have been those used by Massachusetts and Rhode Island, New York, Ohio, Georgia, and Iowa. Another of these old rituals, of which we have a copy, is that of Kentucky, which was printed in 1879 under the title of the *Kingless Tribe*. It is a cipher work. A copy is in the Library of the Supreme Council of the Ancient and Accepted Scottish Rite in Washington. To complete this phase of the study will require a concentrated search to locate, if possible, copies of all these old rituals.

The legend of the origin and development of the present Grand Encampment ritual is based upon the old "Webb Work." The story runs that Webb and others took the then existing ritual, rewrote it in a dramatic form and also included certain features which are typical of our ritual today. Rather extensive and intensive searches have been made at various times to locate a copy of the original "Webb Work." So far these searches have failed to produce results. At about the time of the adoption of the national ritual, the Grand Commandery of Massachusetts and Rhode Island presented a manuscript copy of their ritual to the Grand Encampment for use in adopting a ritual. The ritual thus

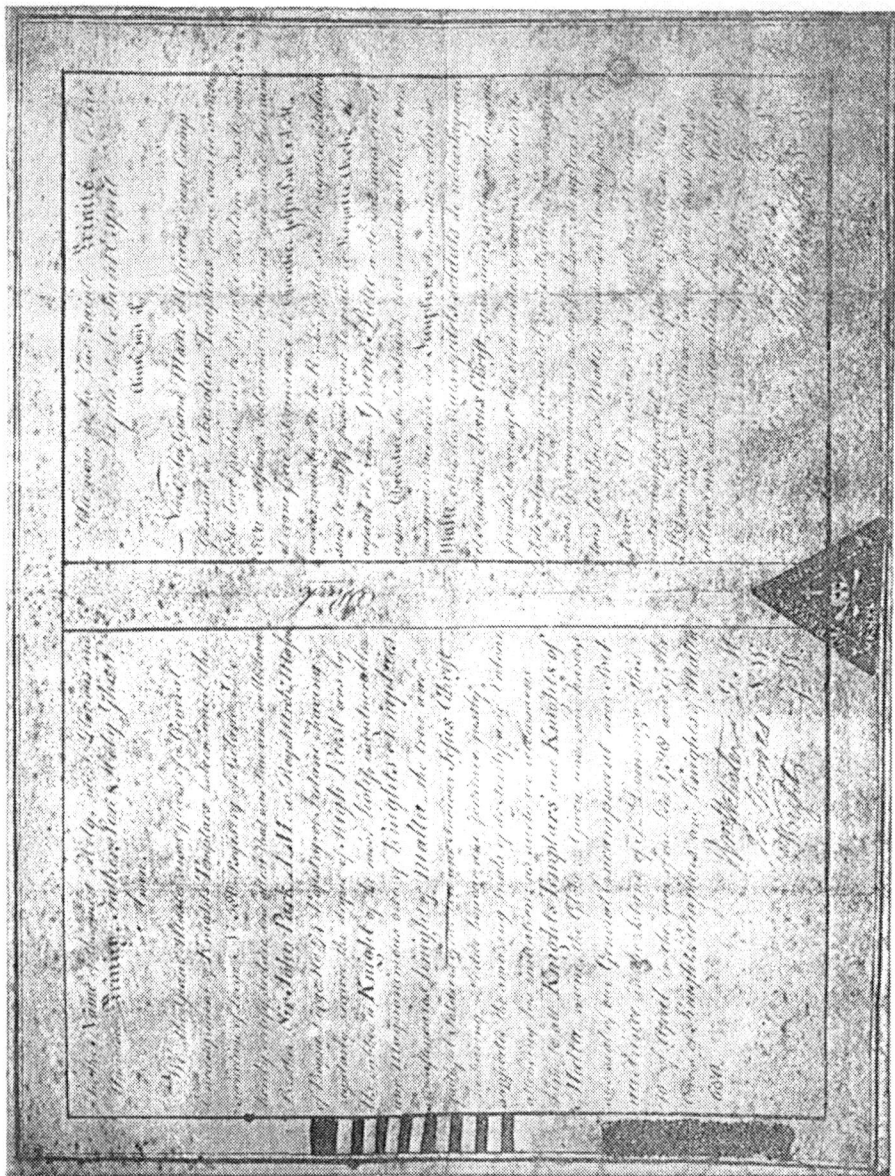

BILINGUAL TEMPLAR DIPLOMA
Templar Diploma in English and French, issued at Port au Prince, Santo Domingo (now Haiti)
and dated April 10, 1798.
(Original now in possession of the Grand Encampment, U. S. A.)

presented was supposed to be the pure "Webb Work" and every evidence points to this as being correct. This manuscript is now lost. Sir Knight Charles Lamb, Past Grand Commander of Wisconsin, has conducted a prolonged search for this ritual but thus far without satisfactory results.

A renewal of this search has begun recently. In the history of the Grand Commandery of Connecticut, published in its Proceedings for the year 1923, there is a statement that a copy of the Webb ritual was one of the cherished possessions of Washington Commandery No. 1, of Hartford. The Grand Commandery of Connecticut is now making a search of all records and papers in the State in an effort to locate this ritual.

Another ritual, which was in use at one time in the United States and which is now lost, is that used by the Pennsylvania Commanderies from 1790 to 1824. This ritual is reported to have been an English ritual. Sir Knight Alfred Creigh, Past Deputy Grand Commander of Pennsylvania, reported that he had a copy of this ritual. This copy has not been found.

Foreign Rituals

The study of rituals other than those used in the United States has just been started. A number of rituals in use at various times in the several parts of the British Empire have been located and copies of some of them obtained. There still remain a number to be located. Among these is the old ritual of the "Cross of Christ Encampment." This ritual dates from about 1790. References to it in the literature of Templary indicate that it may be a fundamental ritual from which most of the others have developed. Evidence has also been found to indicate that a copy was at one time in the archives of the Sovereign Great Priory of Canada. Recent search has failed to produce the ritual. However, through the courtesy of Most Eminent Knight R. V. Harris, Past Supreme Grand Master, the search is still being continued.

CONSTITUTION

OF THE

General Grand Encampment

OF

KNIGHTS TEMPLARS,

AND THE

APPENDANT ORDERS,

FOR THE

UNITED STATES OF AMERICA.

BOSTON:
T. W. White, Printer.
1817.

TITLE PAGE OF THE FIRST PRINTED CONSTITUTION OF THE GRAND ENCAMPMENT, U. S. A. (1817)

Another interesting ritual is that used by the Encampment at Valletta, Malta, in 1849. The notebook from which this ritual was copied also contains a copy of the English ritual adopted in 1851 together with a note to the effect that the latter ritual was put into use on instructions received from London. The 1849 Valletta ritual has a great resemblance to our American rituals and may be a link in determining the origin of ours.

One of the most renowned rituals of the English jurisdiction is the "Baldwyn working." All efforts to obtain a copy of this work from England have so far failed. However, a copy of the ritual used by Percy Encampment of Adelaide, South Australia, has been obtained. This has proved to be virtually the same as the Baldwyn working. Percy Encampment was chartered by Baldwyn Encampment in the latter part of the nineteenth century.

Greater difficulty in obtaining a picture of the Scottish story has been encountered. Copies of the rituals used by two governing bodies in existence in Scotland prior to 1909 have been obtained. These, however, are of comparatively recent date.

A fairly representative picture of the Irish Templar rituals from about 1800 to date has also been completed.

Nothing has yet been done regarding the rituals of the Templar grades of Denmark, Norway and Sweden.

France formerly used the ritual of the Great Priory of Helvetia. Since this Rite operates also in the United States, a discussion of this ritual will not be attempted here. Members of this branch of Templary are known as "Knights Beneficent of the Holy City."

APPENDIX

CALENDAR OF TEMPLAR EVENTS IN THE U. S. A.

[Beginning with the earliest reference to the conferring of the Order of the Temple (August 28, 1769) and extending to the organization of the General Grand Encampment of the U. S. A. (June 21, 1816).]

1769, August 28, Massachusetts, Boston: St. Andrew's Royal Arch Chapter confers the Orders on Brother William Davis.

1769, December 11, Massachusetts, Boston: St. Andrew's Lodge confers the Orders on Paul Revere.

1770, May 14, Massachusetts, Boston: St. Andrew's Lodge confers the Orders on Joseph Warren.

1779, February 7, Pennsylvania, Philadelphia: Thomas Proctor is designated as a Knight Templar in the address prefacing an ode by John Park.

1779, April 14, Mt. Fortune, Island of St. Lucia: Mount Moriah Lodge No. 2 (35th Regt. of Foot) issues certificate (Lodge No. 41) to Philip Crofton as a Sir Knight Templar.

1780, ..., South Carolina, Charleston: An Encampment of Knights Templar organized.

1782, March 3, South Carolina, Charleston: Lodge No. 190 issues a certificate to Donald McPherson stating that he had been dubbed a Knight Templar.

1783, May 27, South Carolina, Charleston: Chapter of Knights of the Red Cross issues certificate to John Steele.

1783, August 1, South Carolina, Charleston: Henry Beaumont receives diploma certifying he has received the degrees of Royal Arch, Knight of Red Cross, Knight Templar, and Knight of Malta, in St. Andrew's Lodge No. 1, Charleston. The seal is of No. 40 which was the number after Pennsylvania rewarranted No. 1 in 1783.

1784, June 30, Halifax, Nova Scotia: John North "installed and dubbed" a Knight Templar by Unity Lodge No. 18, a Pennsylvania Lodge in 17th British Regt. of Foot. It left Philadelphia in 1778.

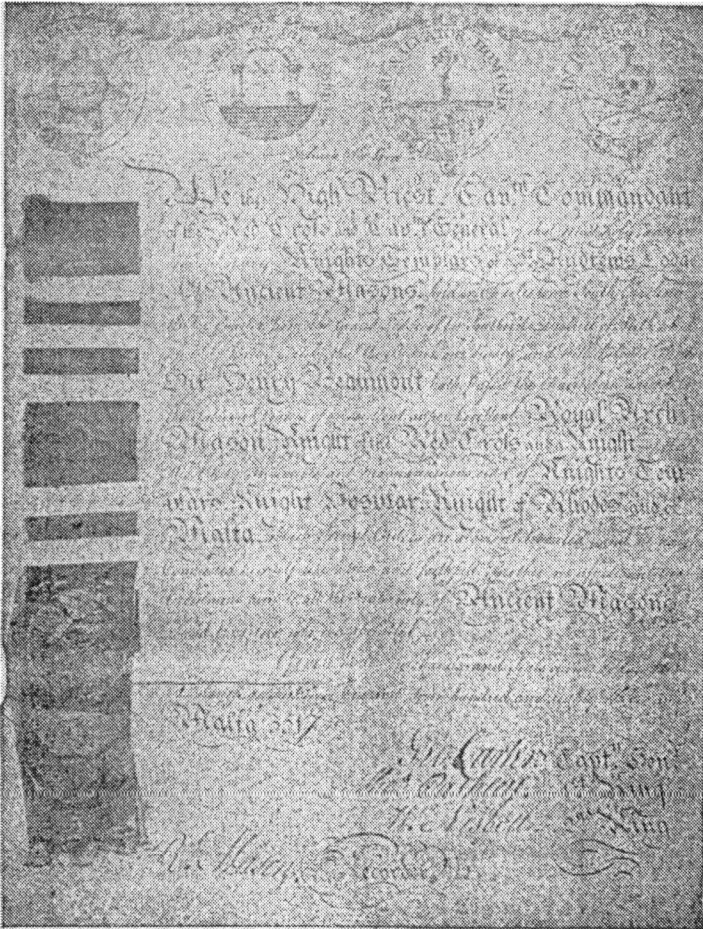

OLDEST AMERICAN TEMPLAR DIPLOMA

The above Patent or Diploma, certainly the oldest of its kind in America, was issued to Brother Sir Henry Beaumont by the High Priest and Captain Commandant of the Red Cross and Captain General of that most holy and invincible Order of Knights Templar of St. Andrew's Lodge No. 1, Ancient Masons of Charleston, South Carolina, on the first day of August, 1783. The diploma which was discovered by Brother Albert G. Mackey, M. D., bears upon it a star of seven points with the name of Deity in center and the motto "Memento Mori"; the Royal Arch on two pillars, the "All Seeing Eye" on its keystone and "Holiness to the Lord" for its motto; a cross and brazen serpent over a bridge and the motto "Jesus Salvator Hominis"; and a skull and crossbones surmounted by a cross and the motto "In Hoc Signo Vinces". Thus by this document one may establish connection between Symbolic Masonry, the Royal Arch, and Templary.

1785, December 27, New York, New York: Knights Templar attend services on St. John's Day in St. George's Chapel.

1786, January 24, Savannah, Georgia: The Hight Priests and Officers of the Royal Arch Chapter and King, Governor and General of the Order of the Red Cross, "in an illustrious grand Chapter, (under sanction of Lodge No. 42 on the Registry of Pennsylvania,)" certify that Ulric Tobler, Past Master, was initiated "into that sublime Degree of an Excellent, Super Excellent, Royal Arch Mason" and "into the Mysteries and regularly dubbed a Knight of the Red Cross."

1789, March 20, Massachusetts, Boston: St. Andrew's Lodge confers the Orders on Benjamin Hurd, Jr.

1789, May 28, Massachusetts, Boston: St. Andrew's Chapter confers the Orders on Elisha Sigourney.

1789, June 24, New York, New York: Knights Templar participate in the festival of St. John and attend services at St. Paul's Chapel.

1789, ..., North Carolina, Wilmington: Edward Jones and Gabriel Kingsbury listed as Knights Templar on the rolls of St. John's Lodge.

1790, October 21, Massachusetts, Boston: St. Andrew's Lodge secures a plate for printing purposes on which are represented Templar emblems, designed by Sir Benjamin Hurd, Jr.

1790, ..., Maryland, Baltimore: An Encampment of Knights Templar organized.

1793, ..., Pennsylvania, Philadelphia: An Encampment of Knights Templar organized.

1794, February 14, Pennsylvania, Philadelphia: Encampment No. 1 confers Orders on John A. Thompson.

1794, July 11, Pennsylvania, Philadelphia: Encampment No. 1 confers the Orders on Andrew Wilson.

1794, September 24, Massachusetts, Boston: St. Andrew's Lodge confers the Orders on Robert Harris, William Francis, and Ebenezer Perkins, of Newburyport.

1794, ..., Massachusetts, Boston: St. Andrew's Royal Arch Chapter discontinued conferring the Order of Knight Templar and Knight of Malta.

1795, January 28, Massachusetts, Boston: St. Andrew's Lodge confers the Orders on Henry Fowle.

1795, June 26, New York, New York: Knights Templar participate in the ceremonies on St. John's Day.

1795, September 11, Pennsylvania, Philadelphia: Encampment No. 1 confers the Orders on David Irving.

1795, ..., Massachusetts, Newburyport: An Encampment of Knights Templar organized.

1796, February 16, Massachusetts, Newburyport: Newburyport Encampment issues a diploma to Hamilton Moore certifying that he had received the Orders of Knighthood.

1796, June 10, Pennsylvania, Philadelphia: Encampment No. 1 confers the Orders on George A. Baker.

1796, July ...., Connecticut, Colchester: An Encampment of Knights Templar hailing from three different Encampments.

1796, ..., New York, Albany: Temple Encampment organized at Albany by John Hanmer, Thomas S. Webb, Gideon Farman, Ezra Ames, and others.

1796, ..., New York, New York: Officers of Old Encampment for the year were Jacob Morton, Grand Master, John Abrams, Generalissimo, Martin Hoffman, Captain General.

1797, February 2, Massachusetts, Boston: The Encampment of Knights of the Red Cross "permitted to make their records in the book of St. Andrew's Chapter."

1797, March 11, Massachusetts, Newburyport: Sir Jonathan Gage and eight other Knights Templar attend the funeral of Brother Benjamin Perkins.

1797, May 12, Pennsylvania, Philadelphia: Convention of Knights Templar met in Philadelphia for the purpose of forming a Grand Encampment. A committee consisting of four representatives from ' each encampment was appointed for the purpose of preparing a constitution.

1797, May 19, Pennsylvania, Philadelphia: Constitution, prepared by a committee composed of four delegates from each of the Encampments represented in the convention of May 12, 1797, adopted and a Grand Encampment of Pennsylvania duly formed.

1797, ..., Pennsylvania, Carlisle: The Orders conferred on John Johnston.

1797, ..., New York, New York: Jacob Morton re-elected Grand Master of Old Encampment.

1797, September 12, United States: Thomas Smith Webb, *The Freemason's Monitor,* lists the following Encampments:

Grand Encampment, Philadelphia
Encampment No. 1, Philadelphia
Encampment No. ...., Philadelphia
Encampment No. ...., Harrisburg
Encampment No. ...., Carlisle
Encampment No. ...., Stillwater
Encampment No. ...., New York City.

1798, ..., New York, New York: Jacob Morton re-elected Grand Master of Old Encampment.

1799, January 14, Pennsylvania, Carlisle: Lodge No. 56 issues a diploma to Jonathan Wallace certifying that he has received the Orders of Knighthood. (Knight Templar, Knight of Malta, Ark Mark Link, Knight of the Mediterranean Pass, Knight of the Red Cross.)

1799, December 16, New York, New York: The Orders conferred on William Richardson.

1799, December 30, New York, New York: Knights Templar instructed to assemble for the ceremonies in eulogy of General George Washington.

1799, ..., New York, New York: Officers of St. Peter's Encampment for the year: John West, Grand Master, Thomas Megan, Generalissimo, Alexander Stewart, Captain General, T. H. Kennedy, Thomas Holmes, and Robert Steele, Standard Bearer.

1799, ..., New York, New York: Jacob Morton re-elected Grand Master of Old Encampment.

1800, January 9, Rhode Island, Providence: Knights Templar participate in ceremonies in eulogy of General George Washington.

1800, June 24, Connecticut, New London: Knights Templar participate in the dedication of Freemason's Hall.

1800, November 12, Pennsylvania, Philadelphia: The Orders conferred on James Aston, Hugh Tearney, Joseph Brobston.

1800, ..., New York, New York: John West re-elected Grand Master of St. Peter's Encampment.

1800, ..., New York, New York: Jacob Morton re-elected Grand Master of Old Encampment.

1801, June 9, Connecticut, New London: Orders conferred in Washington Encampment.

1801, June 10, Connecticut, New London: Washington Encampment adopts by-laws agreeing to meet alternately in Colchester and New London.

1801, November 12, Connecticut, New London: Orders conferred in Washington Encampment.

1801, ..., New York, New York: John West re-elected Grand Master of St. Peter's Encampment.

1801, ..., New York, New York: Jacob Morton re-elected Grand Master of Old Encampment.

1802, March 12, Massachusetts, Boston: An Encampment of Knights of the Red Cross organized.

1802, August 23, Rhode Island, Providence: An Encampment of Knights Templar organized.

1802, September 27, Rhode Island, Providence: Henry Fowle of Boston visits St. John's Encampment.

1802, September 29, Rhode Island, Providence: Orders conferred in St. John's Encampment.

1802, October 10, Rhode Island, Providence: Orders conferred in St. John's Encampment.

1802, October 19, Rhode Island, Providence: Orders conferred in St. John's Encampment.

1802, ..., New York, New York: Jacob Morton re-elected Grand Master of Old Encampment.

1803, June 24, Massachusetts, Newburyport: John Park, a Knight Templar, delivered the address on St. John's Day before St. Peter's and St. John's Lodges.

1803, November 1, Rhode Island, Providence: Orders conferred in St. John's Encampment.

1803, ..., New York, New York: Jacob Morton re-elected Grand Master of Old Encampment.

1804, March 28, Massachusetts, Boston: The Orders conferred on Robert Cash.

1804, June 23, Rhode Island, Providence: Orders conferred in St. John's Encampment.

1804, September 23, Rhode Island, Providence: Orders conferred in St. John's Encampment.

1804, ..., New York, New York: Jacob Morton re-elected Grand Master of Old Encampment.

1805, January 21, Connecticut, Colchester: Washington Encampment elects officers.

1805, May 6, Rhode Island, Providence: Convention of Knights Templar assemble to form a Grand Encampment.

1805, May 13, Rhode Island, Providence: Convention of Knights Templar adopts a constitution and declares the Grand Encampment duly formed.

1805, May 15, Massachusetts, Boston: Thomas Smith Webb verbally reports the formation of the Grand Encampment.

1805, June 24, Massachusetts, Reading: Benjamin Gleason, a Knight Templar, delivered the address on St. John's Day before Mount Moriah Lodge.

1805, August 23, Maine, Portland: An Encampment of Knights of the Red Cross organized by Stephen Foster and others.

1805, September 2, Rhode Island, Providence: St. John's Encampment decides to request a Charter of Recognition from the Grand Encampment.

1805, September 11, Massachusetts, Boston: A communication from the Grand Encampment requests that the Encampment of Red Cross be formed into an Encampment of Knights Templar.

1805, October 7, Rhode Island, Providence: St. John's Encampment receives a Charter of Recognition from the Grand Encampment.

1805, October 9, Maine, Portland: Council of Knights of the Red Cross elects officers. Sir John Coe elected R. S. and S. M.; Stephen Foster elected Secretary. The Encampment voted to petition the Grand Encampment of the Northern States for a Charter of Recognition.

1805, December 16, Rhode Island, Providence: Orders conferred in St. John's Encampment.

1805, December 21, Massachusetts, Boston: Encampment of Knights Templar and Knights of Malta established in Boston; Henry Fowle elected Grand Master.

1805, December 21, Massachusetts, Boston: Boston Encampment of Knights Templar established.

1805, December 25, Connecticut, Colchester: By-laws amended to require candidates to deposit ten dollars with the petition.

1805, ..., Maryland, Havre de Grace: An Encampment of Knights Templar organized.

1806, February 21, Pennsylvania, Philadelphia: Orders conferred in Encampment No. 1.

1806, March 3, Rhode Island, Providence: Grand Encampment meets.

1806, March 3, Massachusetts and Rhode Island Grand Commandery: Issues a Charter of Recognition to Boston Encampment.

1806, March 15, Massachusetts, Boston: Boston Encampment of the Red Cross agrees, since a Grand Encampment of Knights Templar had been formed, to dissolve and transfer its furniture, jewels, and regalia to the Encampment of Knights Templar organized in Boston.

1806, May 6, Connecticut, Colchester: Orders conferred on five candidates.

1806, May 10, Maine, Portland: Encampment of Red Cross at Portland votes to send Sir Stephen Foster to the meeting of the Grand Encampment at Boston, Massachusetts, to request a Charter of Recognition.

1806, May 21, Rhode Island, Providence: Orders conferred in St. John's Encampment.

1806, May 29, Massachusetts, Boston: Grand Encampment meets.

1806, May 29, Massachusetts and Rhode Island Grand Encampment: Issues a Charter of Recognition to a Council (King Darius) of Knights of the Red Cross at Portland, Maine.

1806, August 6, Rhode Island, Providence: Orders conferred in St. John's Encampment.

1806,   September 15, Pennsylvania, Philadelphia: Grand
        Lodge strikes from By-Laws of Lodge No. 101
        "the words 'Knight Templars,' no such being sanc-
        tioned by this Grand Lodge as being a degree in
        Masonry."

1806,   October 6, Maine, Portland: Encampment of
        Knights of the Red Cross adopts the title, King
        Darius Council.

1806,   October 13, Maine, Portland: King Darius Council
        instructs Sir Stephen Foster, Secretary, to apply
        to Sir Otis Ammidon, Grand Recorder, for a
        Charter of Recognition.

1806,   December 22, Maine, Portland: Charter of Recog-
        nition received by King Darius Council.

1807,   January 5, Pennsylvania, Philadelphia: Dr. George
        Green complains that although Grand Lodge "dis-
        avow taking any Cognizance of the proceedings
        of a Society of people called Knights Templars,"
        a room is rented to them; that they "impose upon
        Masons and draw them into their Society under
        pretense of its being a high Degree of Masonry."

1807,   February 23, Maine, Portland: Charter of Recog-
        nition accepted by King Darius Council of Knights
        of the Red Cross.

1807,   February 23, Maine, Portland: King Darius Coun-
        cil of Knights of the Red Cross adopts a code of
        By-Laws.

1807,   May 14, Rhode Island, Providence: Orders con-
        ferred in St. John's Encampment.

1807,   May 28, Massachusetts, Boston: Grand Encamp-
        ment meets.

1807,   June 6, Rhode Island, Providence: Orders con-
        ferred in St. John's Encampment.

1807,   August ...., (Third Thursday), Connecticut, Col-
        chester: Orders conferred on six candidates.

1808, ..., New York, New York: Rising Sun En-
        campment in existence. (See Longworth's Direc-
        tory, New York, 1808-9. It also appears in is-
        sues of 1809-10, 1812-13.)

1808, ..., New York, New York: James McDon-
        ald is Grand Master of Rising Sun Encampment.

1808,   May 12, Rhode Island, Providence: Grand En-
        campment meets.

1808, May 12, Massachusetts and Rhode Island, Grand Encampment: Issues a Charter of Recognition to the Encampment at Newburyport.

1808, October 17, Pennsylvania, Philadelphia: Dr. George Green complains to Grand Lodge that he was "surrounded, and borne down by the persecuting spirit of the Templars." He says: "I am sorry to say that my persecutors, the Templars, do not appear to possess virtue enough to do me justice. I, therefore, wash my hands of them, and may God of His infinite and unbounded mercy, turn their hearts, visit them with repentance, and enter not into judgment with them."

1808, December 25, Rhode Island, Providence: Orders conferred in St. John's Encampment.

1809, January 16, Pennsylvania, Philadelphia: Report to Grand Lodge that Knights Templars Encampment owes "5 years Rent" to December 27, 1807, "which must be against the $100 they had loaned to the Grand Lodge."

OLD TEMPLAR SEAL

This Seal of Knights of the Red Cross, Knights Templar and Knights of Malta was upon a Diploma of St. Andrew's Lodge No. 1, Charleston, South Carolina, which was issued in 1783. (See page 68.)

1809, March 16, Pennsylvania, Philadelphia: Orders conferred in Encampment No. 1.

1809, May 29, Massachusetts, Newburyport: Grand Encampment meets.

1809, September 7, Rhode Island, Providence: Orders conferred in St. John's Encampment.

1809, ..., New York, Ithaca: An Encampment organized.

1810, April 6, Connecticut, New London: "Voted: This Encampment do establish the Charter by them received from London to be the Charter by which they hold and exercise the right of making Knights Templar."

1810, May 31, Massachusetts, Boston: Grand Encampment meets.

1810, July 20, Pennsylvania, Philadelphia: Orders conferred in Encampment No. 1.

1810, October 19, Pennsylvania, Philadelphia: Orders conferred in Encampment No. 1.

1810, December 10, Rhode Island, Providence: Orders conferred in St. John's Encampment.

1810, December 10, New York, New York: Columbian Encampment organized.

1811, ..., New York, New York: Stephen B. Beekman is Grand Master of Rising Sun Encampment.

1811, January 18, Pennsylvania, Philadelphia: Orders conferred in Encampment No. 1.

1811, April 19, Pennsylvania, Philadelphia: Orders conferred in Encampment No. 2.

1811, April 22, Rhode Island, Providence: Orders conferred in St. John's Encampment.

1811, May 27, Rhode Island, Providence: Grand Encampment meets.

1811, May 27, Massachusetts and Rhode Island, Grand Encampment: A committee, consisting of Sir Thomas Smith Webb, Sir John Carlile, and Sir Ephraim Bowen, appointed to correspond with other encampments relative to cooperation with the Grand Encampment.

1811, June 21, Pennsylvania, Philadelphia: Orders conferred in Encampment No. 1.

1811, August 16, Pennsylvania, Philadelphia: Orders conferred in Encampment No. 1.

1811, August 24, Pennsylvania, Philadelphia: Grand Lodge fixes meeting of Encampment for 3rd Saturday and rent at $30 per annum.

1811, September 20, Pennsylvania, Philadelphia: Orders conferred in Encampment No. 1.

1811, December 9, Pennsylvania, Philadelphia: Orders conferred in Encampment No. 1.

1811, December 19, Pennsylvania, Philadelphia: Orders conferred in Encampment No. 1.

1812, March 12, Pennsylvania, Philadelphia: Orders conferred in Encampment No. 1.

1812, April 4, Delaware, Wilmington: Orders conferred in Encampment No. 1.

1812, April 11, Delaware, Wilmington: Orders conferred in Encampment No. 1.

1812, April 17, Pennsylvania, Philadelphia: Orders conferred in Encampment No. 1.

1812, May 4, Delaware, Wilmington: Orders conferred in Encampment No. 1.

1812, May 28, Massachusetts and Rhode Island, Grand Encampment: Committee, appointed at preceding annual conclave to correspond with other encampments relative to the formation of a Grand Encampment, reports progress and asks for permission to continue its duties.

1812, June 1, Pennsylvania, Philadelphia: Petition to Grand Lodge by Encampment No. 1 that 3rd Friday be allotted for their meetings instead of 3rd Saturday, granted.

1812, June 5, Rhode Island, Providence: Orders conferred in St. John's Encampment.

1812, August 21, Pennsylvania, Philadelphia: Orders conferred in Encampment No. 1.

1812, October 16, Pennsylvania, Philadelphia: Orders conferred in Encampment No. 1.

1812, November 20, Pennsylvania, Philadelphia: Orders conferred in Encampment No. 1.

1812, December 18, Pennsylvania, Philadelphia: Orders conferred in Encampment No. 1.

1812, December 27, Pennsylvania, Philadelphia: Thomas Black elected Grand Master of Encampment No. 1.

1812, December 27, Pennsylvania, Philadelphia: Encampment No. 2 united with Encampment No. 1.

1812, December 27, Pennsylvania, Philadelphia: Orders conferred in Encampment No. 1.

1812, ..., Virginia, Winchester: An Encampment of Knights Templar organized.

1812, ..., Massachusetts, Boston: Grand Encampment meets.

1813, ..., New York, New York: Michael Hughes is Grand Master of Rising Sun Encampment.

1813, January 15, Pennsylvania, Philadelphia: Orders conferred in Encampment No. 1.

1813, March 19, Pennsylvania, Philadelphia: Orders conferred in Encampment No. 1.

1813, April 6, Pennsylvania, Philadelphia: Orders conferred in Encampment No. 1. (?)

1813, April 16, Pennsylvania, Philadelphia: Orders conferred in Encampment No. 1.

1813, May 21, Pennsylvania, Philadelphia: Orders conferred in Encampment No. 1.

1813, May 27, Massachusetts, Boston: Grand Encampment meets.

1813, June 18, Pennsylvania, Philadelphia: Orders conferred in Encampment No. 1.

1813, June 21, Rhode Island, Providence: Orders conferred in St. John's Encampment.

1813, June 27, Rhode Island, Providence: Orders conferred in St. John's Encampment.

1813, August 20, Pennsylvania, Philadelphia: Orders conferred in Encampment No. 1.

1813, September 17, Pennsylvania: Encampment No. 1 issues certificate to James McDevitt as a Knight Templar and Knight of Malta.

1813, November 29, Delaware, Wilmington: Orders conferred in Encampment No. 1.

1813, December 28, Delaware, Wilmington: Orders conferred in Encampment No. 1.

1814, January 10, Rhode Island, Providence: Orders conferred in St. John's Encampment.

1814, January 21, Pennsylvania, Philadelphia: Orders conferred in Encampment No. 1.

1814, February 2, Pennsylvania, Pittsburgh: Encampment No. 2, Pittsburgh, formed by brethren who had received the degree of Knights Templar in Lodge No. 45.

1814, February 2, Pennsylvania, Pittsburgh: Orders conferred in Pittsburgh Encampment. (?)

1814, February 15, Pennsylvania, Philadelphia: Convention of Knights Templar convened in Philadelphia to form a Grand Encampment.

1814, February 16, Pennsylvania, Grand Encampment: Convention of Knights Templar in Philadelphia adopted the Constitution as reported by the committee and officers elected.

1814, February 18, Pennsylvania, Philadelphia: Orders conferred in Encampment No. 1.

1814,   March 7, Pennsylvania, Grand Encampment: Committee of the Grand Encampment requests the Grand Lodge of Pennsylvania to rent them a room for a meeting place and to furnish the Grand Encampment with a list of rejections and suspensions. Committee also presents the Grand Lodge with an abstract of the proceedings of the Grand Encampment.

1814,   March 18, Pennsylvania, Grand Encampment: Nathaniel Dilhorn presents a bill for thirty dollars for engraving a seal for the Grand Encampment.

1814,   March 18, Pennsylvania, Philadelphia: Orders conferred in Encampment No. 1.

1814,   April 8, New York, New York: Orders conferred in Rising Sun Encampment.

1814,   April 8, New York, New York: Committee, consisting of M. Hughes, Archibald Bull, and James McDonald, appointed by Rising Sun Encampment to petition the Grand Encampment of Pennsylvania for a Charter of Recognition.

1814,   April 12, Pennsylvania, Pittsburgh: Encampment at Pittsburgh petitions the Grand Encampment for a Charter of Recognition.

1814,   April 13, Pennsylvania, Grand Encampment: Issues a Charter of Recognition to Encampment No. 1 at Philadelphia.

1814,   April 13, Pennsylvania, Philadelphia: John Glenn elected Grand Master of Encampment No .1.

1814,   April 13, Pennsylvania, Philadelphia: Orders conferred in Encampment No. 1.

1814,   April 13, Pennsylvania, Philadelphia: Encampment No. 1 petitions Grand Encampment of Pennsylvania for a Charter of Recognition.

1814,   April 15, Pennsylvania, Philadelphia: Orders conferred in Encampment No. 1.

1814,   April 20, Maryland, Baltimore: Encampment of Knights Templar, meeting in St. John's Lodge room, instructs Archibald Dobbin, Recorder, to request a Charter of Recognition from Pennsylvania. In the letter requesting the charter, Dobbin states the Encampment at Baltimore has been in existence since 1790.

1814, May 2, Pennsylvania: Grand Encampment issues a
Charter of Recognition to Encampment No. 1 at
Philadelphia.

1814, May 2, Pennsylvania, Grand Encampment: Issues a
Charter of Recognition to the Encampment at
Pittsburgh.

1814, May 2, Pennsylvania, Grand Encampment: Issues a
Charter of Recognition to the Encampment at
Baltimore, Md.

1814, May 2, Maryland, Baltimore: Philip P. Eckel
elected Grand Master of Encampment No. 1.

1814, May 3, New York, New York: Elias Dolb elected
Grand Master of Rising Sun Encampment.

1814, May 3, Pennsylvania, Grand Encampment: Issues
a Charter of Recognition to Rising Sun Encampment at New York City.

1814, May 13, Delaware, Wilmington: Encampment at
Wilmington petitions the Grand Encampment of
Pennsylvania for a Charter of Recognition.

1814, May 13, Delaware, Wilmington: Archibald Hamilton elected Grand Master of Washington Encampment.

1814, May 17, Pennsylvania, Grand Encampment: Issues
a Charter of Recognition to the Encampment at
Wilmington, Delaware.

1814, May 20, Pennsylvania, Philadelphia: Alphonso C.
Ireland elected Grand Master of Encampment
No. 1.

1814, May 24, Pennsylvania, Pittsburgh: Francis Bailey
elected Grand Master of Pittsburgh Encampment.

1814, June 6, New York, New York: Thomas Durry,
Recorder of Rising Sun Encampment, reports
that the Encampment is flourishing.

1814, June 7, Maryland, Baltimore: Samuel Cole appointed to represent the Encampment at Baltimore at the Grand Encampment in Philadelphia.

1814, June 7, Massachusetts, Boston: Grand Encampment meets.

1814, June 7, Delaware, Wilmington: Orders conferred
in Encampment No. 1.

1814, June 17, Pennsylvania, Philadelphia: Orders conferred in Encampment No. 1.

1814, June 18, New York, Grand Encampment: Organized at New York City. (The history of Columbian Commandery gives the action of the Sovereign Grand Consistory, etc., as January 22, 1814.)

1814, July 6, Pennsylvania, Grand Encampment: Grand Recorder receives the dues, $15.50, to the Grand Encampment.

1814, July 15, Pennsylvania, Philadelphia: Orders conferred in Encampment No. 1.

1814, September 1, New York, New York: Knights of Columbian Encampment and members of New York Lodges work in a body on the fortifications in Brooklyn.

1814, September 19, New York, Brooklyn: Fort Masonic completed by the Knights of Columbian Encampment and the Lodges of New York.

1814, December 16, Pennsylvania, Philadelphia: Orders conferred in Encampment No. 1.

1815, February 19, Maryland, Baltimore: Sir Philip P. Eckel reports to Sir George Baker, Grand Recorder of the Grand Encampment of Pennsylvania, that, due to invasion of the enemy, the Encampment at Baltimore had been unable to meet.

1815, February 20, Delaware, Wilmington: Orders conferred in Washington Encampment No. 1.

1815, March 24, New York, New York: Orders conferred in Rising Sun Encampment.

1815, May 3, Maryland, Baltimore: Philip P. Eckel re-elected Grand Master of Encampment No. 1.

1815, May 8, Delaware, Wilmington: Archibald Hamilton re-elected Grand Master of Washington Encampment.

1815, May 8, Delaware, Wilmington: Orders conferred in Washington Encampment No. 1.

1815, May 13, Maryland, Baltimore: Philip P. Eckel re-elected Grand Master of Encampment No. 1.

1815, May 17, New York, New York: Elias Dolb re-elected Grand Master of Rising Sun Encampment.

1815, May 19, Pennsylvania, Philadelphia: Samuel Black elected Grand Master of Encampment No. 1.

1815, May 20, Pennsylvania, Pittsburgh: Francis Bailey re-elected Grand Master of Pittsburgh Encampment.

1815, May 22, New York, New York: Columbian Encampment petitions the Grand Encampment of New York for a Charter of Recognition.

1815, June 1, Maryland, Baltimore: Orders conferred in Encampment No. 1.

1815, June 6, New York, New York: Orders conferred in Rising Sun Encampment.

1815, June 7, New York, New York: Orders conferred in Rising Sun Encampment.

1815, June 9, New York, New York: Orders conferred in Rising Sun Encampment.

1815, June 10, New York, New York: Orders conferred in Rising Sun Encampment.

1815, June 10, Pennsylvania, Grand Encampment: Meets in Philadelphia. William McCorkle elected General Grand Master.

1815, June 26, Rhode Island, Providence: Grand Encampment meets.

1815, June 26, Pennsylvania, Pittsburgh: Charter of Pittsburgh Encampment No. 2 returned to the Grand Encampment by Sir Andrew Scott, Generalissimo.

1815, June 27, Rhode Island, Providence: Orders conferred in St. John's Encampment.

1815, August 8, Pennsylvania, Philadelphia: Orders conferred in Encampment No. 1.

1815, August 10, Delaware, Wilmington: Orders conferred in Washington Encampment No. 1.

1815, September 15, Pennsylvania, Pittsburgh: Orders conferred in Pittsburgh Encampment.

1815, September 15, Pennsylvania, Philadelphia: Orders conferred in Encampment No. 1.

1815, November 13, Delaware, Wilmington: Orders conferred in Washington Encampment No. 1.

1815, ..., Louisiana, New Orleans: An Encampment of Knights Templar organized.

1816, February 4, New York, Grand Encampment: Issues a Charter of Recognition to Columbian Encampment as No. 5.

1816, February 12, Delaware, Wilmington: Orders conferred in Washington Encampment No. 1.

1816, February 16, Pennsylvania, Philadelphia: Several knights of Encampment No. 1 request the right to form an Encampment in Philadelphia to be known as No. 3.

1816, February 16, Pennsylvania, Grand Encampment: Issues a Charter to Encampment No. 3 in Philadelphia.

1816, February 23, Rhode Island, Providence: Orders conferred in St. John's Encampment.

1816, March 15, Pennsylvania, Philadelphia: Orders conferred in Encampment No. 1.

1816, March 17, Pennsylvania, Philadelphia: Orders conferred in Encampment No. 1.

1816, March 24, Virginia, Richmond: St. John's Rising Star Encampment of Virginia formed by a convention of Knights Templar.

1816, March 27, Pennsylvania, Philadelphia: Encampment No. 3 constituted.

1816, March 27, Pennsylvania, Philadelphia: Thomas Hennessey elected Grand Master of Encampment No. 3.

1816, April 8, Delaware, Wilmington: Orders conferred in Washington Encampment No. 1.

1816, May 4, New York, Grand Encampment: Issues a warrant for the formation of Indivisible Friends Encampment No. 6, at New Orleans, Louisiana.

1816, May 5, Maryland, Baltimore: Adam Denmead elected Grand Master of Encampment No. 1.

1816, May 13, Delaware, Wilmington: Archibald Hamilton re-elected Grand Master of Washington Encampment.

1816, May 15, Massachusetts, Boston: Grand Encampment meets.

1816, May 15, Massachusetts and Rhode Island, Grand Encampment: Appoints Sir Knights Thomas Smith Webb, Henry Fowle, and John Snow to represent the Grand Encampment at the General Convention of Knights Templar in Philadelphia.

1816, May 16, New York, New York: Elias Dolb re-elected Grand Master of Rising Sun Encampment.

1816, May 16, Pennsylvania, Philadelphia: Orders conferred in Encampment No. 1.

1816, May 17, Pennsylvania, Philadelphia: John L. Baker elected Grand Master of Encampment No. 1.

1816, May 23, Massachusetts, Boston: Boston Encampment authorizes a loan to the Grand Encampment to send delegates to a convention of Knights Templar to be held in Philadelphia during June, 1816.

1816, June 9, Pennsylvania, Grand Encampment: Meets in Philadelphia. Joseph Barnes elected General Grand Master.

1816, June 9, New York, Grand Encampment: Meets to select a delegate to the convention of Knights Templar at Philadelphia.

1816, June 10, New York, Grand Encampment: Issues credentials to Sir Thomas Lowndes as delegate to convention of Knights Templar in Philadelphia.

1816, June 10, Pennsylvania, Grand Encampment: Issues credentials to Sir Knights William McCorkle, Archibald Hamilton, Benjamin Edes, and Alphonso C. Ireland, as delegates to the convention of Knights Templar.

1816, June 11, Pennsylvania, Philadelphia: Delegates from Pennsylvania, Massachusetts, and Rhode Island assemble in Philadelphia to consider the formation of a General Grand Encampment.

1816, June 11, Pennsylvania, Grand Encampment: Meets and Committee reports conference with delegates from the New England Grand Encampment and a delegate from a Grand Encampment in New York, and give their opinion that the establishment of a General Grand Encampment would greatly tend to promote Union, Order, and Strength amongst Knights Templar.

1816, June 12-13, Pennsylvania, Philadelphia: Convention in session.

1816, June 14, Maryland, Baltimore: Orders conferred in Encampment No. 1.

1816, June 14, Pennsylvania, Philadelphia: Orders conferred in Encampment No. 1.

1816, June 14, Pennsylvania, Philadelphia: Delegates unable to agree on methods of organization and of working Orders, so adjourn.

1816, June 16, Pennsylvania, Grand Encampment: Meets and delegates report meeting and deliberation with delegates from New England and New York, and their discovery "that it was impossible to carry their designs into execution, without making a sacrifice upon the part of this Grand Encampment and its Subordinate Encampments, which was considered to be unwarranted by every principle of Masonry; which was made a *sine qua non* with the Delegates from New England," and consequent dissolving of the Convention.

1816, June 20, New York, New York: Delegates from New York, Massachusetts, and Rhode Island reconvene to consider proposals for the formation of a General Grand Encampment.

1816, June 21, New York, New York: The General Grand Encampment of Knights Templar of the United States of America organized.

PREFACE TO FIRST EDITION.

To the Officers and Members of the Independent Order of Good Templars in North America:

At the last session of the Right Worthy Grand Lodge, held at the city of Indianapolis, in May last, the following Resolutions were adopted, viz:—

"Resolved,—That our R. W. G. Templar, S. B. Chase, be appointed to arrange, prepare and print a Digest of the Rules and Usages of the Order, together with the Decisions of the R. W. G. Lodge.

"Resolved,—That the R. W. G. T. be requested to publish the Constitution and By-Laws of this R. W. G. Lodge, together with the amendments which have been adopted thereto, and have the same printed with the Digest.

"Resolved,—That the R. W. G. Templar is hereby permitted to have said Digest and Constitution printed at his own cost, and allowed to retain the proceeds of the sale of the same as a full compensation for said services."

In obedience to the above resolutions, I have prepared a Digest of the Rules and Usages of the Order, embracing our Constitution, By-Laws, Decisions of the R. W. G. Lodge, R. W. G. Templars, Grand Lodges and G. W. C. Templars, and Rules of Order, with a very brief Manual of Practice under them, with a complete index to the whole work.

S. B. CHASE,

R. W. G. Templar,

Great Bend, Pa., Oct. 1, 1859.

CONSTITUTION

OF

RIGHT WORTHY GRAND LODGE.

PREAMBLE.

WHEREAS, at the Annual Session of the Grand Lodge of North America, held at Ithaca, in December, 1853, it was deemed advisable that upon the institution of five or more Grand Lodges of the I. O. of G. T., measures should be taken to organize a National Lodge, and at the session of said Grand Lodge held at Corning, in December, 1854, the proper number of Grand Lodges having been instituted, provisions were made for the organization of a supreme head of the Order; and believing that the cause of temperance and the interest of this Order will be advanced by organizing such an institution as shall unite under one general head the various organizations of this Order: We, the Representatives, in Convention assembled, do ordain and make the following form of Constitution, By-Laws and Rules of Order, for the government of this Grand Lodge:

ARTICLE I.

SEC. 1. This Lodge shall be known by the name, style and title of the R. W. GRAND LODGE OF THE INDEPENDENT ORDER OF GOOD TEMPLARS.

SEC. 2. It is the source of the true and legitimate Order of Good Templars in North America, and possesses such powers and jurisdiction over the whole Order as are provided in the Constitution and in the Ritual of the same. Its authority extends also to such Lodges as may be organized under its Charter in foreign countries.

SEC. 3. By virtue of Charters granted by it, all State, District, and Territorial Grand Lodges exist, and with it rests the power, by a majority of two-thirds of the votes cast, to deprive such State, District, or Territorial and Provincial Grand bodies of their Charters, and annul their authority; *Provided*, that such deprivation or annulment shall only be made for violation of the laws of this R. W. Grand Lodge. No more than one Grand Lodge shall be chartered in any State, District, or Territory. All Grand bodies working under charters granted by this Grand Lodge are supreme for all local legislation and appellate jurisdiction within their respective limits, except as hereinafter provided.

SEC. 4. With the consent of the Grand Lodge of a State, District or Territory, an appeal may be had by any Subordinate Lodge to this R. W. Grand Lodge, such consent, however, not being necessary where an expelled Lodge, after having surrendered up to its Grand Lodge all its effects, appeals from the decision thereof. But in all cases the decision of the State, District, Territorial, Provincial or Country Grand Lodges shall be final and conclusive, until reversed by this Grand Lodge on a direct appeal thereof.

SEC. 5. To this Grand Lodge belongs the power to regulate and control the unwritten work of the Order, and to fix and determine the customs and usages in regard to all things which appertain thereto; and to it alone belongs the power to provide and establish suitable lectures and other written work therefor. But the unwritten work of the Order shall in nowise be altered or amended except with the concurrence of four-fifths of the members present of this Grand Lodge at its annual session.

SEC. 6. To this Grand Lodge is reserved the power to establish the Independent Order of Good Templars in such countries, domestic or foreign, wherein the same has not been established.

SEC. 7. To this Grand Lodge belongs the immediate jurisdiction over all subordinate Lodges in such countries, domestic or foreign, as are without Grand Lodges.

SEC. 8. To it belongs the power to enact all laws of general application to the order.

SEC. 9. All power and authority in the Order not reserved to this Grand Lodge by this Constitution, are truly vested in the various State, District and Territorial Grand Lodges.

ARTICLE II.

This Grand Lodge shall be composed of its Officers and Representatives, and Past Officers and Representatives, from the several State, District, Territorial, Provincial and Country Grand Lodges, working under legal and unreclaimed charters granted by the Grand Lodge.

ARTICLE III.

SEC. 1. The elective Officers of this Grand Lodge, shall be R. W. Grand Templar, R. W. Grand Counsellor, R. W. Grand Vice Templar, R. W. Grand Secretary, R. W. Grand Treasurer, who shall be elected by ballot by a majority of all the votes cast annually at the stated session of this Lodge, and shall be installed into their respective offices immediately after their election.

SEC. 2. The appointed officers of the Grand Lodge shall be, R. W. G. Chaplain, R. W. G. Marshal, R. W. G. D. Marshal, R. W. G. I. Guard, R. W. G. O. Guard, who shall be nominated by the R. W. G. T., and if approved of by the Grand Lodge, shall be installed into their respective offices immediately after the installation of the elective officers.

SEC. 3. Should any of the elective officers fail to appear to be installed at the time provided, the particular office or offices shall be declared vacant, and the Grand Lodge shall, in the event, proceed to a new election to fill such vacancy or vacancies, and the officer or officers so elected shall be accordingly installed.

SEC. 4. It shall be the duty of the officers, both elective and appointed, to attend each meeting of the Grand Lodge, and perform such duties as are enjoined by the laws and regulations of the Order, and such as may be required by the presiding officer, and shall receive such compensation as hereinafter provided.

SEC. 5. All members shall be eligible to office and vote on all questions, except the election of officers, and when the yeas and nays are called, and shall be permitted to take part in the proceedings and debates of this Grand Lodge.

ARTICLE IV.

SEC. 1. The R. W. G. T. shall preside at all meetings of the Grand Lodge, preserve order and enforce the laws thereof. He shall have the casting vote whenever the Lodge shall be equally divided, other than upon a ballot for officers, but shall not vote on any other occasion. He shall appoint all committees not required to be raised by ballot, and all District Deputy Grand Templars for States, Districts, Territories or Countries where there is no Grand Lodge.

During the recess of this Grand Lodge, he shall have a general superintendence of the interests of the Order. He may hear and decide such appeals as may be submitted to him by the several State Grand Lodges, or by Subordinate Lodges under the immediate jurisdiction of this Grand Lodge. He may hear and decide such questions other than questions arising out of the Constitution of the several State, District, Territorial, Provincial or Country Grand Lodges as may be submitted to him by the several State, District, Territorial, Provincial or Country Grand Lodges, or the Grand Worthy Chief Templars thereof, or by the Grand Representatives, or by the Subordinate Lodges under the immediate jurisdiction of this Grand Lodge. And his decision in all appeals and questions so submitted to him shall be binding on the Lodges or persons submitting the same, until reversed by this Grand Lodge. He is empowered to receive petitions and grant charters for the opening of Grand or Subordinate Lodges, and all charters so granted by him shall be of force until recalled by this Grand Lodge. At every annual session of this Grand Lodge he shall make a report in writing of all his acts and doings, including all his official decisions during the recess in relation to the official business transacted by him.

SEC. 2. During his term of service he shall not hold any office in any State, District, Territorial, Provincial or Country Grand or Subordinate Lodge.

SEC. 3. In case of the removal of the R. W. G. T. from office, or of his death, resignation or inability to discharge the powers and duties of the said office, the same shall devolve on the R. W. G. Counsellor for the unexpired term, and in case of the death, removal, resignation or inability of both R. W. G. T. and R. W. G. C., the duties of the office shall devolve upon the R. W. V. T., and the Grand Lodge at the first session succeeding thereto shall proceed to elect and install a R. W. G. T. and R. W. G. C. for the unexpired term.

ARTICLE V.

The Right Worthy Grand Counsellor shall open and close the meetings of the Grand Lodge, support the R. W. G. T. by his counsel and assistance, and preside in his absence. In case of the removal, death or resignation of the R. W. G. T., the powers and duties of said office shall devolve on the R. W. G. C. for the unexpired term, as provided in Sec. 3 Art. IV.

ARTICLE VI.

The R. W. V. T. shall assist the R. W. G. T. in conducting the business of the Grand Lodge, he shall have special charge of the door, and in the absence of the R. W. G. T. and R. W. G. C., he shall preside, and in case of a vacancy in both these offices, he shall perform the duties of R. W. G. T. as provided in Sec. 3, Art. IV.

ARTICLE VII.

The R. W. G. Secretary shall make a just and true record of all the proceedings of the Grand Lodge in a book provided for that purpose, keep the journal of all secret sessions, and preserve and keep the evidences of the unwritten work of the Order, and such alterations as may from time to time be made therein, and all other records pertaining to the work of the Order, and the explanations and lectures relating thereto ; summon the members to attend all special meetings ; keep accounts between the Grand Lodge and the Grand and Subordinate Lodges under its jurisdiction ; receive all moneys belonging to this Lodge, and pay the same to R. W. G. T. without delay, taking a receipt for the same; read all petitions, reports and communications; carry on, under the direction of the Grand Lodge or R. W. G. T., its correspondence, and transact such business of the Grand Lodge, appertaining to his office, as may be required of him by the Grand Lodge. All communications transmitted or received by him officially shall be laid before the Grand Lodge. He shall receive for his service such compensation as the Grand Lodge shall, from time to time, determine.

ARTICLE VIII.

SEC. 1. The Grand Treasurer shall keep the moneys and all the evidences of debt, choses in action, deeds, &c., of the Grand Lodge, and pay all orders drawn on him by the R. W. G. T., attested by the Grand Secretary, and under the seal of the Grand Lodge. He shall lay before the Grand Lodge, at its stated annual session, a full and correct statement of his accounts. Before his installation, he shall give a bond, with two sureties, to the Grand Lodge, in such sum as may from time to time be fixed, and shall receive such compensation as the Grand Lodge shall determine.

SEC. 2. No money shall be drawn from the Treasury but in consequence of appropriations made by the Grand Lodge.

ARTICLE IX.

SEC. 1. The Grand Chaplain shall perform such duties as appertain to his office, and as may from time to time be required by the Grand Lodge relative thereto.

SEC. 2. The Grand Marshal shall assist the R. W. G. T. in performing his duties in such manner as he may from time to time be required, and perform all the duties generally appertaining to his office.

Sec. 3. The R. W. G. D. Marshal shall perform such duties as appertain to his office.

Sec. 4. The R. W. G. Guards shall perform such duties as are required of them by the laws and usages of the Order.

ARTICLE X.

Sec. 1. The Grand Representatives shall be chosen by the several State, District, Territorial, Provincial and Country Grand Lodges, for the term of one year. And if vacancies occur by death, resignation or otherwise, during the recess of the Grand Lodge of any State, District, Territory or Country, such vacancies shall be filled in the manner pointed out by the Constitution of such State, District or Territorial Grand Lodge.

Sec. 2. The basis of representation shall be as follows, viz: Every State, District or Territorial Grand Lodge, having under its jurisdiction less than one thousand members, one representative; for one thousand members, two representatives; for five thousand members, three representatives; for twenty thousand members and more, four representatives. No State, District, Territorial or Country Grand Lodge shall have more than four representatives.

Sec. 3. A Grand Representative must be a member of a Subordinate Lodge in good standing; he must have received the third degree, and be in possession of the Grand Lodge degree; he must reside in the State, District, Territory, Province or Country where the Grand Lodge he represents is located. No representative shall represent more than one Grand body at the same time.

Sec. 4. Grand Representatives shall be furnished by the Grand body they represent with such certificates as shall be required by law.

Sec. 5. In case of contested elections, this Grand Lodge shall determine to whom the contested seat belongs.

ARTICLE XI.

Sec. 1. This Grand Lodge shall have the power, a

majority consenting thereto, to impeach and try any of its officers or members, and with the concurrence of two-thirds of the votes cast, to expel from officership or membership therein any officer or member so impeached and tried.

SEC. 2. During the trial of any impeachment, the officer or member under impeachment shall be debarred from the exercise of his office or the privilege of his membership, but may be heard in his own defence.

SEC. 3. Suspension or expulsion from the Subordinate Lodge of which an officer or member of this Grand Lodge is a member, shall *ipso facto* work a suspension from officership or membership in this Grand Lodge, and the vacancy thereby created shall be filled in the manner hereinbefore described.

ARTICLE XII.

This Grand Lodge shall meet annually on the fourth Tuesday in May, at 10 o'clock, A. M., at such place as the Grand Lodge may from time to time determine. It may also meet on its own adjournment. It may also meet specially on the call of the R. W. G. T., of which he shall cause one month's notice to be given to the representatives of the several State, District, Territorial, Provincial or Country Grand Lodges, communicating to them the purpose for which the special meeting is called, and in no case shall any business be transacted at a special meeting, unless notice thereof has been given, as above stated.

ARTICLE XIII.

SEC. 1. Representatives from a majority of the whole number of State, District, Territorial, Provincial and Country Grand Lodges shall be necessary to form a quorum for the transaction of business, but a smaller number may adjourn from day to day, and may receive and act upon the credentials of new members, except in contested elections.

SEC. 2. This Grand Lodge shall be the judge of the certificates, or returns and qualifications of its members.

SEC. 3. It may determine the rule of its proceedings and from time to time adopt such rules of order as it may see fit.

SEC. 4. A journal of its proceedings shall be kept, and published annually, except such proceedings as shall be had in secret session.

SEC. 5. Voting for officers shall be by ballot, and should there be more than two candidates for the same office after the second ballot, the candidate on each subsequent balloting having the lowest number of votes shall be dropped until an election is made.

SEC. 6. All other voting shall be *viva voce* or by yeas and nays, as the Grand Lodge may require; the yeas and nays may be demanded by one-fifth of the members present, and shall be entered upon the journal.

SEC. 7. All questions shall be decided by a majority vote, except in such cases as a specific majority is required.

ARTICLE XIV.

SEC. 1. The revenues of this Grand Lodge shall be as follows: Fees for Charters for Grand Lodges or Subordinate Lodges working under its immediate jurisdiction, viz: $15 for Grand Lodge Charters and Rituals, $8 for Charters, Rituals and Cards for Subordinate Lodges, and $3 for Charters, Rituals and Cards for Degree Temples.

SEC. 2. Dues from State, District or Territorial Grand Lodges, $30 per annum for each vote they shall be entitled to in this Grand Lodge, *provided*, that Grand Lodges with a membership less than two thousand shall only be required to pay $30.

SEC. 3. Dues from Subordinate Lodges, working under the immediate jurisdiction of this Grand Lodge, five cents per capita, to be paid quarterly.

SEC. 4. Proceeds of the sales of books, cards, diplomas, odes and certificates.

ARTICLE XV.

SEC. 1. To be an officer of this Grand Lodge, one nominated must have received the Grand Lodge degree, and be a member in good standing of a Subordinate Lodge.

SEC. 2. Candidates for the several elective officers

may be nominated by the State, District, Territorial, Provincial or Country Grand Lodges or by the Grand Representatives.

SEC. 3. The nominations and election of Grand officers shall take place on the same day, to wit: the second day of the annual sessions. The nominations for each office shall be immediately succeeded by the election for the same, and before the nominations and elections for the next office.

ARTICLE XVI.

SEC. 1. The members of this Order from each State, District, Territory, Province or Country, under jurisdiction of this Grand Lodge, shall be entitled to admission into the Lodges of every other State, District, Territory, Province or Country, upon proving themselves according to the established work of the Order, and the production of a proper card.

SEC. 2. No citizen of one State, District, Territory, Province or Country wherein Lodges are established, shall be admitted to membership in a Lodge of another State, District, Territory or Province or Country, without the previous consent of the Grand Lodge of the State, District or Territory whereof such citizen is a resident.

SEC. 3. A member of the Order, suspended from a Lodge in any State, District, Territory, Province or Country, shall not be admitted to membership in a Lodge of another State, District, Territory, Province. or Country, without the previously obtained consent of the Lodge from which he is suspended.

SEC. 4. All persons becoming members of this Order shall be required to subscribe to the following pledge, viz: That they will not make, buy, sell or use, as a beverage, any spirituous or malt liquors, wine or cider, and will discountenance the manufacture and sale thereof in all proper ways.

ARTICLE XVII.

The officers and members of this Grand Lodge, (except such officers as receive stated salaries,) shall receive a compensation for their services, to be ascertained by law, and paid out of the treasury of this Grand Lodge,

ARTICLE XVIII.

By-Laws in conformity with this Constitution may be made, which shall not be altered or amended, unless such amendment shall be proposed at a stated annual session, and acted upon at the same session, but not on the day on which it is offered, and adopted by two-thirds of the votes given.

ARTICLE XIX,

This Constitution and the By-Laws which shall be made in pursuance thereof, shall be the supreme law of the Order, and shall be binding upon the State, District, Territorial, Provincial and Country Grand Lodges under the jurisdiction of this Grand Lodge.

ARTICLE XX.

This Constitution shall not be altered or amended, except a proposition therefor be made in writing, signed by one or more Representatives from three different Grand Lodges, and entered upon the journal, at a regular Annual Session. At the next regular Annual Session, after being so offered, such proposition shall be considered, and shall be subject to amendment, alteration or postponement by a majority vote of the Representatives present; and upon its final passage, if agreed to by two-thirds of the Representatives present, on a call of the yeas and nays, such proposition or amendment thereof, shall become part of this Constitution.

BY-LAWS.

ARTICLE 1. Upon the petition of ten members of the Order, or ten respectable citizens of any town or place, praying for a charter to open a Subordinate

Lodge in a State, District, Province, Country or Territory where there has not been established a Grand Lodge, this Lodge may grant the same. Each Subordinate Lodge receiving a Charter from the Grand Lodge, shall be opened by a member regularly deputized therefor by the R. W. G. T., who shall deliver to such Lodge the Charter and Charge Books, and shall, at the opening thereof, give the necessary instruction. Such Lodge shall be visited at least once a year by the R. W. G. T., or by a District Deputy G. T.

ART. 2. Subordinate Lodges working under the immediate jurisdiction of this Grand Lodge, shall transmit to the Grand Secretary quarterly reports, containing the same information as is required from Grand Lodges by Art. 8 of these By-Laws. The report shall be accompanied by the dues in current money.

ART. 3. Ten or more Subordinate Lodges, located in any State, District, Province, Country or Territory, where a Grand Lodge has not been established, may petition this Grand Lodge in writing, praying for the charter of a Grand Lodge, which, if approved by a majority of the votes given, shall be granted, and such Grand Lodge shall be opened by the R. W. G. T., or by some qualified brother, who shall be specially deputized for that purpose.

ART. 4. All travelling or other expenses incurred in opening a Grand or Subordinate Lodge, shall be paid by such Lodge.

ART. 5. Applications for Grand or Subordinate Lodges shall be accompanied by the fee for the same, which shall be returned if the charter is not granted.

ART. 6. Each Grand Lodge shall have a Grand Seal; an impression thereof, in wax, or an electrotype thereof, shall be sent to the R. W. G. Secretary, and deposited in the archives of this Lodge.

ART. 7. The Constitution of each Grand, and By-Laws of each Subordinate Lodge, chartered by this Lodge, immediately on its adoption, shall be forwarded to this Lodge for approval.

ART. 8. Annual returns shall be made by each G. L. under the jurisdiction of this Grand Lodge, in which they shall give the names of Grand Officers; and 1st, number last report; 2d, number initiated; 3d, admitted by card; 4th, restored; 5th, retired on clearance cards; 6th, withdrawn from the Order; 7th, suspended; 8th, expelled; 9th, deaths; 10th, full degree members; 11th, in good standing. Said returns shall be made to the R. W. G. Secretary, at least one month previous to the annual meeting of this body, and shall be accompanied with the dues thereon, in money current at par in the place where the meeting of this body is to be held.

ART. 9. No person shall, at the same time, hold membership in more than one Grand or Subordinate Lodge, nor shall any Lodge initiate a person who has been elected a member of a sister Lodge, or confer the degrees on members of other Lodges, without the consent of such Lodges, given under its seal.

ART. 10. When a Grand Lodge shall be duly chartered in any State, District, Territory, Province or Country, all the Lodges in said District, State, Territory, Province or Country working under the jurisdiction of this Grand Lodge, shall thereafter be declared subordinate to, and under the jurisdiction of, the Grand Lodge of the State, District, Territory, Province or Country in which they are located, and no Lodge situated in one State, District, Territory, Province or Country, can be made subordinate to the Grand Lodge of any other State, District, Territory, Province or Country.

ART. 11. No member can be allowed to visit a Lodge out of the State, District, Territory, Province or Country where he resides, unless he presents a certificate or card under the signature of the officers and the seal of the Lodge of which he is a member, and signed on the margin in his own proper hand-writing, and prove himself in the T. P. W., and in the degree in which the Lodge is open. *Provided*, nevertheless, a member may always visit if introduced by a Grand Representative or other elective Grand Officer, or vouched for by a member of the Lodge he proposes to visit.*

---

* Contrary to this article, Indiana (5th s., 14) and some other Grand Lodges, have decided that *vouching* for members is not known in our

ART. 12. At each annual session, the R. W. G. T. shall appoint in each State, District, Territory, Province and Country in which there is not a Grand Lodge, an officer to be styled D. D. G. W. T., whose duty it shall be to act as the special agent of this Grand Lodge in relation to the matters herein specified, viz:

1st. To act for the R. W. G. T., and by his direction perform whatever may have been ordered to be done by the Grand Lodge in the particular district for which he is approved.

2d. To act as the representative of this Grand Lodge, and perform all such matters relating to the Order in his district as the R. W. G. T. shall direct.

3d. To obey all special instructions of the R. W. G. T. in relation to anything that officer is required to do for the good of the Order.

4th. To act as the agent of the Grand Secretary, and obey the special instructions of that officer.

5th. To have general supervision over all Subordinates (in his district) which work under charters granted by this Grand Lodge.

6th. To make quarterly reports of his acts and doings to R. W. G. T. His decisions of law and order shall be binding upon Subordinates, until reversed by R. W. G. T. or this Grand Lodge.

7th. He shall in no case interfere as an officer of this Grand Lodge with State Grand Lodges.

8th. To qualify a brother for the appointment of D. D. G. T., he must be a contributing member of a Subordinate Lodge, and must have attained the rank of P. W. C. T., or be able to pass a satisfactory examination in the work of the first, second and third degrees. His appointment shall be for one year, but may be revoked for cause at any time by the R. W. G. T.

9th. The Deputy instituting a new Lodge, shall appoint a suitable person as Deputy for said Lodge, and

---

Order, and that W. C. T's, should never allow it. Such Grand Lodges must have strangely lost sight of this By-Law, to make so unconstitutional a decision. Such decisions are null and void, unless they confine their operations to visiting Lodges within the jurisdiction of the Grand Lodge so making them. In such case, the decision is legal and binding, as Grand Lodges can control and regulate visiting between Lodges and members of their own jurisdiction.—R. W. G. T. CHASE.

shall report his name to the R. W. G. S. with the institution returns.

ART. 13. The Representatives of each Grand Lodge shall be examined by the W. G. M. as to their qualifications for the office, previous to taking seats in this Grand Lodge, and on taking their seats, each shall be furnished by the Grand Secretary with a copy of the Constitution, Rules of Order, and Laws of the Grand Lodge.

ART. 14. Each Grand Lodge shall furnish its Representatives all documents and papers necessary in the discharge of the duties of their office.

Art. 15. Each Grand Lodge shall be furnished with one hundred copies of the proceedings of this R. W. G. L., and as many more as they have Subordinate Lodges under their jurisdiction.

ART. 16. All dues and moneys for this Grand Lodge shall be paid to the Grand Secretary, and by him be paid over to the Grand Treasurer, taking his receipt for the same. It shall be the duty of the R. W. G. S. on the first day of the session of this R. W. G. L., to make a full and complete written report of the number of Subordinate Lodges working under the jurisdiction of this Grand Lodge, and where located ; the name and number of Grand Lodges ; the number of Subordinate Lodges under the jurisdiction of each Grand Lodge, together with all his official and financial acts.

ART. 17. No Grand or Subordinate Lodge under the jurisdiction of this Grand Lodge, shall adopt or use, or suffer to be adopted or used in their jurisdiction, any other charges, lectures, degrees, ceremonies, forms of installation or regalia, than those prescribed by this Grand Lodge. All sessions of Grand and Subordinate Lodges shall open and close with prayer.

ART. 18.—§ 1. *Form.* The **Regalia** of this order shall be collars about twenty-two inches in length, *maximum*, and about sixteen inches, *minimum*, narrow at the neck, and wide at the bottom, with the outer corner rounded off.

§ 2. COLORS. The *first* or *initiatory* degree, shall be *white*. The *second* or degree of *Fidelity*, shall be *blue*. The *third* or degree of *Charity*, shall be *purple*. *Officers* of *Sub-Lodge*, scarlet, with *lace* or *fringe*. *Officers* of *Degree-Lodge* or Temple, *purple*. Deputies, *purple*. The *Grand Lodge Degree* shall be *scarlet*. *Officers* and *Members* of the R. W. G. Lodge, *scarlet*, with a small *purple* collar, or band attached.

§ 3. ROSETTES. The Rosette of this Order shall be *white ground*, *blue* and *scarlet* centre, with *yellow star*, or button.

§ 4. EMBLEMS. *Official Emblems*, in all branches of the Order, shall be a *gilt wreath*, enclosing *silver letters*, on blue or purple ground, designating the official title of the wearer; worn on the left breast.

Representatives may wear the number of their Lodge, or the abbreviated names of the State from which they are sent, on the right breast. It shall be discretionary to use the emblems or not.

§ 5 TRIMMINGS. *Initiatory*, or *first degree* regalia, requires no other than the rosette, but if other trimmings are desired, they should be of *white* or *silver*.

For *second degree*, or blue regalia, *silver*, and for *third degree*, or purple, *gilt*, and for *Officers* of *Sub-Lodge*, either gilt or silver.

For *Officers* of *Degree Lodge*, or Temple, and for all *Deputies*, G. Lodge and R. W. G. Lodge regalia, gilt trimming shall be used. The quality and amount of trimming shall be left to the taste or option of the Lodges or members. But Deputies, G. Lodge and R. W. G. Lodge regalia, shall be fully trimmed with *lace*, *stars* or embroidery, *emblems*, *fringes* and *tassels*. All members shall be entitled to wear, in any meeting of the Order, the regalia of the highest degree, or position, to which they have attained.

ART. 19. The R. W. G. T. shall appoint the following committees, to consist of three members: Committee on State of the Order, Legislative Committee, Committee on Correspondence, Committee on Finance, on Appeals, Constitutions, Petitions, Credentials, Returns, Printing, Mileage and Per Diem, and such Special Committees as are authorized by the Grand Lodge and not otherwise provided for.

ART. 20. The T. P. W. is designed only for the use of members who are traveling beyond the limits of the jurisdiction to which they belong, and in order that each member may be properly instructed in it, and visiting members properly examined, the three highest elective officers of a Lodge are to be privately put in possession of the word at the time of their installation, that they may be qualified either to give or receive it. The G. W. C. T. and G. W. C. and G. W. V. T. and the regular D. D. G. C. T. should also be in possession of it.

Art. 21. The fiscal year of this Grand Lodge commences on the first day of May, in each year.

Art. 22. The Charters of all Subordinate Lodges immediately under the jurisdiction of this Lodge, which fail to make their returns for one year, shall be forfeited, and whenever such remissness shall occur, the R. W. G. T. shall take proper means to enforce this law.

ART. 23. This Grand Lodge will neither entertain nor consider any inquiry as to what are the laws and usages of the Order, unless the same be brought before the body by an appeal from the decision of a Lodge, or unless the same be presented by a Grand Lodge.

Constitutions for Grand and Subordinate Lodges.

AUTHORITY.

The following is the uniform Constitution adopted at the session of R. W. G. Lodge, held at Detroit, May, 1867, for Grand and Subordinate Lodges, which, according to the vote of that body, is to be the fundamental law for all Grand Lodges hereafter organized, and Subordinate Lodges under the jurisdiction of such Grand Lodges, as well as for all Subordinate Lodges under the immediate jurisdiction of the R. W. G. Lodge: also to be in force within the jurisdiction of all Grand Lodges heretofore organized, whose Grand bodies have not procured a supply of printed Constitutions for their Grand and Subordinate Lodges. Grand Lodges now in existence are invited to examine it, and adopt the same, if receiving their approval.

GENERAL RULES.

To avoid ambiguity of expression, the masculine form of the pronoun is used in the following pages, and generally in all Good Templar publications, but it is in all cases to be construed as referring to either sex, according to circumstances.

No person can be admitted to membership in this Order, unless he believes in the existence of Almighty God as the Ruler and Governor of all things, *and is willing to take our pledge for life;* under this rule we welcome all classes to our Order. The young—that we may save them from falling into the snares of the tempter; the inebriate, *who earnestly desires to reform* —that we may assist him to break the chains of appetite that bind him to the car of ruin; the moral and social—that, by uniting all these elements of society, we may the better advance the cause of Temperance and morality.

Constitution of the Grand Lodge.

SEC 1. NAME.—This Lodge shall be entitled, the Grand Lodge of ——, of the Independent Order of Good Templars.

SEC. 2. JURISDICTION.—This Grand Lodge shall have jurisdiction over all Subordinate Lodges and Degree Temples of Good Templars now existing, or which may hereafter exist in the —— of ——. It shall have the sole right and power to grant, suspend, or revoke charters ; to originate and regulate the means of its own support, and to receive and decide appeals, and determine all questions of law and usage, subject to the R. W. G. Lodge of North America.

SEC. 3. THE MEMBERS of this body shall be its officers and past officers, representatives and past representatives, who are contributing members of the several Lodges subordinate to this Grand Lodge, and who have taken the Grand Lodge Degree, and been admitted, as required by this Constitution.

SEC. 4. THE BASIS OF REPRESENTATION may be regulated by this Grand Lodge in its By-Laws; but, in the absence of such express provision, each Subordinate Lodge shall be entitled to one Representative. Alternate Representatives may be chosen, (if desired,) under such rules as may be prescribed by the Grand Lodge in its By-Laws.

SEC. 5. ELECTION AND TIME OF SERVICE.—The regular election of Representatives shall be held at the first regular meeting in the quarter during which the annual session of the Grand Lodge is held. Written ballots shall be used, and a majority of all votes cast shall be necessary to a choice. If the Lodge fail to elect at the regular time, or if vacancies occur, or a Lodge is entitled to additional Representatives previous to any session, an election may be had at any regular meeting within four weeks of such session. The regular term of service shall be one year; but those elected to fill vacancies, and such additional Representatives as may be elected prior to other than annual sessions, shall serve only until the next annual election. No Lodge can be represented by any but its own members, and a transfer of membership shall vacate a Representative's seat.

SEC. 6. PRIVILEGES OF THE GRAND LODGE.--All acting and past W. C. T.'s, acting and past W. V. T.'s, and all Deputies of the G. W. C. T.. shall be entitled to the G. L. Degree, and all the privileges of membership in this G. Lodge, except voting, provided that they are in good standing in their several Lodges, and present the proper credentials.

SEC 7. CREDENTIALS.—All Representatives shall receive a regularly attested certificate of election to this body. All members entitled to the G. L. Degree, under Sec. 6, shall receive a certificate of services in their respective offices from the Lodge in which said services were rendered, and this shall be their proper credentials entitling them to seats in this Lodge, and the G. W. C. T.'s commission shall be the requisite credentials of deputies. But no Representatives or non-voting members can be admitted, unless they are full Degree members, and in possession of the current quarterly pass-word.

SEC. 8. VOTING.—All members under Sec. 3, of this Article, shall be eligible to office, and vote on all questions except the election of officers, and when the yeas and nays are called, and shall be permitted to take part in the proceedings and debates of this Grand Lodge. The yeas and nays may be demanded on any question, by one-fifth of the members present.

ARTICLE II.—SESSIONS.

SEC. 1. THE ANNUAL SESSION of this Lodge shall commence on the —— day of —— in each year. at —

o'clock, A. M., at such place as the G. Lodge shall have designated. Special meetings may be called by the G. S., when ordered by the G. W. C. T., and shall be so called, on written application of ten members, representing at least seven Lodges. No session shall be opened for general business, unless at least seven Lodges are represented; but a smaller number may open, act on the credentials of members, confer the Grand Lodge Degree, and adjourn from time to time, until a quorum shall be present.

ARTICLE III—OFFICERS.

Sec 1. The Officers of this Lodge shall be, 1st, Grand Worthy Chief Templar; 2d, Grand Worthy Counsellor; 3d, Grand Vice Templar; 4th, Grand Secretary; 5th, Grand Treasurer; 6th, Grand Chaplain; 7th, Grand Marshal; 8th, Grand Guard; 9th, Grand Sentinel; 10th, Assistant Grand Secretary; 11th, Deputy Grand Marshal. The *first five* shall be elected by the Lodge; the 6th and 7th appointed by the G. W. C. T. elect; the 8th and 9th by the G. V. T. elect; the others by the officers they assist. The G. W. C. T. may also appoint a Grand Messenger, when desired by the G. Lodge; he shall also appoint, from time to time, such full Degree members for State, District, County, Special and Lodge Deputies, as the interests of the order may seem to require.

Sec. 2. The Regular Election of Grand Officers shall be by ballot, on the second day of each annual session. The nominations for each office shall be followed by the election of the same, before the nominations for the next, and a majority of all the votes cast shall be necessary to a choice. All officers, unless removed according to the provisions of this Constitution, shall hold their seats until their successors are installed.

Sec. 3. Vacancies in any office may be filled at any session, and in case the office of G. Secretary becomes vacant, the G. W. C. T., by consent of the Executive Committee, shall appoint a member of this Grand Lodge to act in said office until the next session, when the vacancy shall be filled by election, and such appointed officer shall receive the regular salary for the term of such service.

SEC. 4. PENALTIES.--This G.Lodge may place on trial, and remove any officer for dereliction of duty and improper conduct, by a vote of two-thirds of the members present. It may enforce upon its members any penalty, to the extent of expulsion, for a violation of the Constitution, Rules, Obligations, or any of the principles of the Order.

ARTICLE IV—DUTIES OF OFFICERS.

SEC. 1. The G. W. C. T. shall be the chief executive officer of this G. Lodge, and of the Order of Good Templars in this State.' He shall preside at all its sessions, preserve order, enforce a proper observance of the laws and usages of this body, decide questions of doubt or difficulty, whenever properly submitted, appoint such officers and committees as the Constitution or usage may require, provide for the institution of new Lodges and the general prosperity of the Order. He shall be clothed with the power and provided with the means necessary to the thorough and faithful discharge of his duties, submit at each session a full, written report of the work done by himself or deputies, all decisions made, the condition of the Order, its prospects and requirements for the future, and shall discharge such other duties as the interests of the Order require.

SEC. 2. The G. W. C. shall assist the G. W. C. T., preside in his absence or disability and, in case of its vacancy, assume that office and perform its duties until the next session, when a G. W. C. T. shall be elected.

SEC. 3. The G. V. T. shall render such assistance to the G. W. C. T. as may be required, have charge of the doors and ante-rooms of the G. Lodge, and direct the admission of members. In case the office of G. W. C. becomes vacant, he shall assume and perform the duties of the office, and in the absence of the G. W. C. T. and G. W. C. shall preside; and in case of vacancies in both these offices shall act as G. W. C. T. until the succeeding session, when they shall be filled by election.

SEC. 4. The G. S. shall be the recording and corresponding officer of the G. Lodge. He shall keep a cor-

rect record of all its proceedings and of those of the
Grand Council, also of the returns of the Subordinate
Lodges, notify all Subordinate Lodges of the action
of this body, furnish them with such instructions,
blanks, &c., as may be necessary for their correct
working, and furnish for publication the "Journal of
Proceedings," and an abstract of returns, immediately
after each session. He shall be Chairman of the Com-
mitte on Returns and Credentials, with power to make
or direct necessary corrections. He shall keep the
financial accounts of this Grand Lodge, receive its
moneys, and pass the same over to the G. Treasurer,
taking his receipt; but may, when it becomes necessary to make immediate use of the money, pay it upon
the order of the G. W. C. T., and place the order in the
hands of the G. T. At the end of his term, and also
at every session, he shall present a full written report
of the business of his office, with all the information
in his possession relative to the condition of the Order.
He shall prepare and publish the "Journal of Proceedings," Blank Returns, Credentials, Certificates, Circu-
lars, Pass-words, and such other matters as the G.
Lodge shall direct or the interests of the Order require.

SEC. 5. The G. T. shall receive all monies, securities
and vouchers of the G. Lodge and pay all orders
drawn on him by the G. W. C. T. and G. S., and shall
keep an accurate account of his receipts and expendi-
tures, and make a full report in writing at each regular session.

SEC. 6. The G. Messenger shall act as Janitor of the
hall, keep the room and regalia in order, and convey
messages.

SEC. 7. All Grand officers shall discharge such duties
as may be required by the Ritual or usages of the Order, or by the G. Lodge.

SEC. 8. Each Lodge Deputy shall instruct the Lodge
under his charge in the work, and enforce obedience to the rules and usages of the order, collect all
taxes, assessments, bills and returns due the G. Lodge,
and immediately forward them to the G. S.; install
officers and impart the passwords when the quarterly

returns and the G. Lodge tax are placed in his hands, and not otherwise; he shall grant such dispensations as may be authorized by the laws of the Order, and at the close of each quarter furnish the G. W. C. T. with a report of his proceedings and the condition of the Lodge. He shall perform such other duties as are specified in his commission.

SEC. 9. THE EXECUTIVE COMMITTEE shall be composed of the Elective Grand Officers, and any Grand Lodge may, by majority vote, add the Junior P. G. W. C. T. present in the jurisdiction to said Committee. They shall have power to grant and revoke charters and, in the recess of the Grand Lodge, shall exercise the powers of that body, but all their acts shall be subject to be set aside or revised by the G. Lodge.

ARTICLE V—COMMITTEES.

SEC. 1. The G. W. C. T. shall appoint, at each annual session of the G. Lodge, the following committees, to consist of five each, viz:—Committee on Appeals, Committee on Finance, Committee on Credentials and Returns, Committee on State of the Order, Committee on Constitutions.

SEC. 2. The Committee on Appeals shall receive all appeals that may be presented to the G. Lodge at least ten days before any regular session, and report thereon in writing. They shall receive the testimony adduced by the Deputy and no other.

SEC. 3. The Committee on Finance shall examine, audit and report upon all bills and claims presented, and the books and accounts of the officers; at each session report, in writing, the state of the finances, and at each annual session recommend such measures of finance as they may deem necessary.

SEC. 4. The Committee on Credentials and Returns shall examine and report upon all returns, credentials and claims for seats submitted to them.

SEC. 5. The Committee on the State of the Order shall, at each session of the G. Lodge submit a report containing such information as they may deem interesting or instructive. They shall take charge of such reports of officers, resolutions, petitions, &c., as may be referred to them, and recommend such measures as in their judgment will best promote the interests of the Order.

SEC. 6. The Committee on Constitutions shall examine and report on all amendments to the Constitution and By-Laws submitted to them.

ARTICLE VI.—REVENUE.

SEC. 1. The revenue of this body shall be derived from charter fees and supplies required by Subordinate Lodges and Degree Temples, and such *per capita* tax upon the membership of Subordinate Lodges and Degree Temples, fees for each initiation and Degrees conferred, as may be determined and voted at the annual sessions of the Grand Lodge, and such special assessments as may be imposed by a two-thirds vote of the Grand Lodge, at a regular session.

SEC. 2. CHARTER FEES.—The fees for charters and set of Books and Cards shall not be less than ten dollars, and new Lodges and Degree Temples shall pay the necessary expenses of the Instituting Officer.

ARTICLE VII.—SUBORDINATE LODGES.

SEC. 1. CHARTERS.—On the written application of ten or more persons, not less than sixteen years of age, in good standing, in any community, the G. W. C. T. and G. Secretary may grant a charter and designate a Deputy to institute the Lodge, and instruct the members in the work of the Order; provided, however, that no application emanating from a city, town or village in which a Lodge shall then exist, shall be granted without the consent of such Lodge, or if there be more than one Lodge, without the consent of one of such Lodges, except by vote of the Executive Committee or Grand Lodge.

SEC. 2. MEMORIALS, PETITIONS, APPEALS.—All members of Subordinate Lodges shall have the right to memorialize or petition this G. Lodge; also to appeal from the decision of the W. C. T. or Subordinate Lodge to the District Deputy, and if there be no District Deputy, or if his decision is unsatisfactory, then appeals may be taken to the G. W. C. Templar, or Grand Lodge, and these rights shall not be abridged by reason of informality.

SEC. 3. RETURNS.—All Subordinate Lodges shall make returns at the end of each quarter, as full as the forms provided for them permit, and a failure to make such returns for one year shall work a forfeiture of Charter. Deputies instituting new Lodges shall also make full returns, according to the forms provided them.

SEC. 4. SURRENDER OF CHARTER AND BOOKS.—The person having in custody the Charter and books of any Lodge shall surrender them to the Deputy at any time, when ordered to do so by the Executive Committee.

SEC. 5. OFFENSES.—The Executive Committee, on being informed that any Lodge has violated any of the laws of the Order, or is so conducting as to bring reproach upon the Order, shall at once investigate the case, and, if they find the charges sustained, take such measures as they may deem necessary to punish the Lodge and protect the Order. But the Lodge may appeal from the action of the Executive Committee to the Grand Lodge.

SEC. 6. CERTIFICATES.—Members of an extinct Lodge, in good standing at the time of its demise, may at any time within twelve months afterwards, receive from the G. S. a certificate, under his hand and the seal of the G. Lodge, which shall serve the purpose of a clearance card; provided the G. S. may, for good reasons, refuse to grant a certificate to any member, subject to the decision of the Executive Committee.

SEC. 7. RESTORING CHARTERS.—At any time within one year from the surrender of a charter, the Executive Committee may, if they deem it expedient, on such terms as they may determine, restore the Charter, on petition of ten persons who were members of the Lodge, in good standing, at the time of the surrender.

ARTICLE VIII.—JOURNAL, SALARIES, BONDS.

SEC. 1. JOURNAL.—The reports of officers and committees with the approved decisions of the G. W. C. T. and an abstract of returns, shall be published with the "Journal of Proceedings."

SEC. 2. SALARIES.—The G. W. C. T. and G. S. shall be entitled to such salary or remuneration for their services as may from time to time be voted by this G. Lodge.

SEC. 3. BONDS.—The G. Secretary and G. Treasurer shall each, prior to installation, execute to the G. W. C. T., G. W. C. and G. V. T., by names, and to their successors in office, a bond, in such sum as the G. Lodge may name, with two approved sureties, conditioned for the faithful discharge of their official duties, rendering just and true accounts, just payment of all funds coming into their hands, and immediate delivery of all moneys and property belonging to this Grand Lodge, at the close of their term of office.

ARTICLE IX.—BY-LAWS AND AMENDMENTS.

SEC. 1. BY-LAWS.—This G. Lodge may, at any regular session, adopt such By-Laws, Rules of Order, or Order of Business, as may be found necessary, which do not conflict with this Constitution, nor that of the R. W. G. Lodge of N. A. *Provided*, that said By-Laws, or Rules of Order, and all amendments or additions thereto, shall first receive the approval of the R. W. G. Lodge, or in the interim between sessions, the approval of the R. W. G. Templar.

SEC. 2. AMENDMENTS.—This Constitution, and the Constitution of Subordinate Lodges shall be altered or amended only by the R. W. G. Lodge, in the manner provided in Article 20 of the R. W. G. L. Constitution, for the alteration or amendment thereof.

Provided, That at the annual session of this R. W. G. L., in 1870 and 1871, amendments offered on the first day of the session, by direction of any Grand Lodge, or of its Executive Officers, may be acted upon at the same sessions, but not on the same day.

Constitution of Subordinate Lodges, I. O. G. T.

ARTICLE I.—NAME, HOW COMPOSED, QUORUM.

SEC. 1. This Lodge shall be called————Lodge, No.——Independent Order of Good Templars of the ———of———. It shall consist of at least ten members, and cannot surrender its charter so long as that number, in good standing, object thereto. Seven members shall constitute a quorum.

ARTICLE II.—PLEDGE.

SEC. 1. No member shall make, buy, sell, use, furnish, or cause to be furnished to others, as a beverage, any Spirituous or Malt Liquors, Wine or Cider; and every member shall discountenance the manufacture, sale, and use thereof in all proper ways.

ARTICLE III.—MEMBERSHIP.

SEC. 1. ELIGIBILITY.—No person under twelve years of age shall be admitted a member of this Lodge, and the Lodge, by a By-Law, may fix any higher limit not above eighteen years. A person residing in any other town in which a Lodge exists, must have the consent, in writing, of that Lodge, or if more than one Lodge exist there, the consent of one of them.

SEC. 2. PROPOSITION AND BALLOT.—The name, residence, and occupation of a candidate for membership, shall be presented in writing by some member of the Lodge, and referred to a committee of three, two of whom shall be appointed by the W. C. T., and one by the W. V. T. The committee shall investigate the subject, and report thereon at the next regular meeting, when the Lodge shall ballot on the proposition. Four black balls shall be sufficient to reject a candidate, but a vote of rejection may be re-considered on motion of any member, at the same or next meeting, but at no other. The G. W. C. T., or his Deputy, when requested by a vote of two-thirds of the members present, may grant a dispensation to ballot for a candidate on the same evening he is proposed; in their absence, the ballot may be taken by unanimous consent of the Lodge.

SEC. 3. WITHDRAWAL OF PROPOSITION.—A proposition for membership having been referred to a committee, shall not be withdrawn except by a majority vote.

SEC. 4. POSTPONEMENT.—Should the Committee of Investigation find cause, or any member desire it, the report and proposition may be indefinitely postponed, (which shall not be considered a rejection, but a new proposition may be made at any time.)

SEC. 5. DEPOSIT OF CARD.—A candidate for membership by card shall deposit it with the proposition, or furnish satisfactory evidence that it has been lost; and he shall be subject in all cases to the provisions of the second section of this Article.

SEC. 6. EXPELLED AND REJECTED CANDIDATES.—No person who has been expelled or rejected from this or any other Lodge of the Order, shall be again proposed within three months from the date of his expulsion or rejection; and no member who has been suspended shall be proposed for membership in any other Lodge, until he has been re-instated in the Lodge suspending him.

SEC. 7. SIGNING THE CONSTITUTION.—Every person, on becoming a member, shall sign this Constitution.

SEC. 8. Charter members must be initiated within three months of the institution of the Lodge.

ARTICLE IV.—FEES AND DUES.

SEC. 1. INITIATION FEES AND QUARTERLY DUES.— The initiation fee and quarterly dues shall not be less than such amount as may be determined by the Grand Lodge in its By-Laws, to be paid in advance, but no dues shall be required of any one for the current quarter of his initiation.

SEC. 2. PENALTY FOR NON-PAYMENT.—No member shall receive the Pass-Word until his dues for the current quarter are paid. and no member without the Pass-Word shall be permitted to sit in the Lodge.

SEC. 3. DEGREES.—Each Lodge granting a certificate for Degrees to a member, shall not receive less than twenty-five cents for each Degree, which shall go into the funds of the Lodge.

ARTICLE V.—OFFICERS AND TERMS.

SEC. 1. TITLES.—The officers of this Lodge shall be: 1st, Worthy Chief Templar; 2d, Worthy Vice Templar; 3d, Secretary; 4th, Financial Secretary; 5th, Treasurer: 6th, Chaplain; 7th, Marshal; 8th, Guard; 9th, Sentinel; 10th, Assistant Secretary; 11th. Deputy Marshal; 12th, Right Supporter; 13th, Left Supporter. The *first nine* shall be elective, the Supporters appointed by the W. C. T. elect; and the others by the officers they assist.

SEC. 2. ELIGIBILITY.—After this Lodge has been instituted three terms, no member shall be eligible to the office of W. C. T. or W. V. T., unless he has previously served one term in some office, and none but full Degree members shall, at any time, be eligible to either of these offices, after the second election.

SEC. 3. ABSENCE.—If any officer shall be absent from the Lodge for three successive meetings, without rendering, at the expiration of that time, a valid excuse, his seat may be declared vacant by a two-thirds vote.

SEC. 4 VACANCIES.—Vacancies may be filled at any time, and the member holding an office at the close of his term, shall receive the honors of that term. In absence of the W. C. T., the W. V. T. is entitled to preside, and if both W. C. T. and W. V. T. are absent the *senior* P. W. C. T. present. In absence of all entitled to preside. the Secretary, or some other member shall call the Lodge to order, and the Lodge may, by vote in the usual manner, select some member to act *pro tem.* Any officer entitled to the Chair may yield the claim to the G. W. C. T. or his Deputies, or any P. W. C. T.

SEC. 5. TERMS AND ELECTIONS.—The regular terms shall commence with the first meetings in February, May, August and November. The officers shall be elected by ballot and majority vote at the last regular meeting in each term, and installed at the first.

ARTICLE VI.—DUTIES OF OFFICERS.

SEC. 1. P. W. C. T.—The W. C. T. of one term shall be, when present, the acting P. W. C. T. of the succeeding term. In his absence, the P. W. C. T. next in seniority shall fill that office. He shall have an oversight of the ceremonies, correct errors in the signs and instructions, give the charge to initiates as required by the Ritual, and examine and introduce visitors who apply for admission.

SEC. 2. The W. C. T. shall be the chief executive officer of the Lodge, preside at its meetings, enforce a due observance of the Constitution and Laws, exact compliance with the Constitution and Laws of the Grand Lodge, and the usages and ceremonies of the Order, see that all the officers perform their proper duties, appoint all committees and officers not otherwise provided for, inspect and announce the result of all balloting and votes, but shall not vote himself except upon ballot, and in case of tie, when all present have voted. He shall, together with the Secretary, call special meetings when necessary, or when called upon by written application of seven members; sign all drafts, cards and certificates ordered by the Lodge, and see that the returns are made out, and money appropriated for the Grand Lodge tax, and that the bond of the Treasurer elect is made out and approved prior to installation; and perform such other duties as may be required by the Ritual or Lodge properly devolving upon that office.

SEC. 3. The W. V. T. shall render the W. C. T. such assistance as may be required, perform the duties of that office in his absence, and have charge of the doors and ante-rooms of the Lodge.

SEC. 4. The Secretary shall keep a fair and impartial record of the proceedings of the Lodge, write communications, fill up certificates, notify of meetings when ordered by the W. C. T., and attest all moneys ordered to be paid at a regular meeting, and no other. He shall make out, at the end of the term, for the Lodge, a full report of the proceedings during his term, and also the quarterly returns to the Grand Lodge, and with the W. C. T. certify thereto. He shall perform such other duties as may be required of him by the Lodge, or his charge, and deliver up to his successor, within one week from the expiration of his term, all books, papers, or other property in his possession, belonging to his office. He shall immediately notify all neighboring Lodges of the name, occupation and residence of every person rejected, expelled or suspended from this Lodge for any cause except non-payment of dues.

SEC. 5. The F. Secretary shall keep just and true accounts between the Lodge and its members, credit the amounts received, and immediately pay the same over to the Treasurer, taking a receipt. On the evening of the installation he shall present to the Lodge a full report, and furnish the Secretary with the amount of receipts for initiation fees and dues during his term, and with any other information connected with his office necessary to enable the Secretary to prepare correct returns for the Grand Lodge, and shall deliver up to his successor all books, papers, and other property in his possession, belonging to the Lodge. He shall perform such other duties as the Lodge or his charge may require of him.

SEC. 6. The Treasurer shall give a bond of not less than——dollars, with such surety as may be approved by the Lodge, and shall pay all orders drawn on him by the W. C. T., attested by the Secretary, and no others. He shall receive all moneys of the Lodge, and hold the same until the expiration of his term, unless otherwise ordered. He shall keep a full and correct account of all moneys received and expended, and deliver up, when legally called upon, all books. moneys, papers, and other property of the Lodge to his successor in office, or to whomsoever the Lodge may appoint. He shall make a report at the end of his term and perform such other duties as may be required of him by the Lodge or his charge.

SEC. 7. The Marshal shall have charge of the regalia and all other property of the Lodge, which is not specially entrusted to other officers, and see that it is kept

In proper order, and at the close of his term, report a schedule of the same and its condition. He shall assist the W. C. T. in preserving order, superintend the balloting, count the votes upon division, introduce candidates, and perform such other duties as may be required by the Ritual or Lodge.

SEC. 8. The Guard and Sentinel, under direction of the W. V. T., shall have charge of the doors and ante-rooms of the Lodge.

SEC. 9. The A. S. and D. M. shall act under the directions of the S. and M. respectively, and perform such other duties as may be required of them.

SEC. 10. GENERAL PROVISIONS.—The officers shall, in addition to the duties specially laid down in this article, perform such other duties as may be required of them by the Constitution, By-Laws, Rules, Rituals, ceremonies and usages of the Order, or by a vote of the Lodge.

ARTICLE VII.—DEGREES.

SEC. 1. ELIGIBILITY.—A member *eighteen* years of age, one month after his initiation in the First Degree, shall be eligible to the *Second Degree*, and one month after he has received the Second Degree, shall be eligible to the *Third Degree*. No member, not thus qualified, shall receive the Degrees, except Charter members on the institution of a new Lodge, except by *written* dispensation of the G. W. C. T. or his Deputy; which dispensation shall not be given in case of a member under eighteen years of age, only when requested by the unanimous ballot of the Degree members of the Lodge to which such member belongs, or, in case such Lodge shall be connected with a Degree Temple, the unanimous ballot of such Temple.

SEC. 2. APPLICATION AND BALLOT.—Members who desire to receive the Degrees, shall apply for them to the F. S. of the Subordinate Lodge, and pay him the fees therefor. The F. S. shall furnish each applicant with a certificate to that effect, and at the proper time give notice thereof to the Lodge. The applicants shall present their certificates at a Degree meeting of the Lodge, when open in the Degree applied for, when a ballot shall be taken. *Three* black ballots shall reject a candidate, in which case the certificate shall be returned to the candidate, with the rejection and date endorsed thereon, and shall not again be presented under two months, provided the ballot of rejection may be reconsidered at the same meeting on motion of any member. This section shall be in force *only* in Lodges not connected with a Degree Temple.

SEC. 3. Degree meetings shall be held at such times as the Lodge shall determine, (the Lodge Deputy to designate the time if the Lodge fail to do so,) and shall be presided over *only by* the G. W. C. T., his Deputy, or a Degree Templar of some Temple duly chartered and organized ; but it shall be the especial duty of the Lodge Deputy to confer the Degrees, or see that they are duly conferred.

Seven full Degree Members of the Lodge, with the presiding officer, shall constitute a quorum for the conferring of the Degrees, except when conferred on members of a new Lodge by the instituting officer. This section shall be in force *only* in Lodges not connected with a Degree Temple.

SEC. 4. RETURNS TO SUB-LODGES.—The presiding officer at any Degree Meeting held acording to Sec. 3 of this Article, and the Secretary of every Temple. shall, previous to the close of the month within which such officer or Temple has conferred any Degree, forward certificates to the Secretary of the Lodge, giving the name of each member of such Lodge upon whom such officer or Temple has conferred either Degree, and designating the Degree and time when it was so conferred.

SEC. 5. ROLL OF MEMBERS.—The Secretary of each Sub-Lodge shall keep a roll of the members of his Lodge who shall have taken the Second Degree, and a separate roll of those who shall have taken the Third Degree, with the date when each Degree was conferred, and, if the Lodge is connected with a Degree Temple, he shall immediately notify the Temple of the suspension, expulsion, withdrawal from the Lodge or Order, of any of its Degree members, and if a suspended Degree member shall be reinstated, he shall notify the Temple of his reinstatement.

· SEC. 6. FEES AND DUES.—The initiation fee for each Degree shall not be less than twenty-five cents, and an additional fee of fifty cents shall be paid for each dispensation* granted according to Sec. 1 of this Article, to be paid in Sub Lodge at the time of applying for the Degrees, or in Degree Temple when the proposition is presented. The regular dues in Degree Temples shall not be less than *twenty cents* for each annual term, to be paid quarterly in advance. Temples may also charge an admission fee of not more than fifty cents to full Degree members, who may be admitted as members of the Temple, under Sec. 9 of this Article.

SEC. 7. DEGREE TEMPLES.—Upon the application of not less than ten full Degree members, accompanied by the Charter fee, and also a certified vote of the Lodge or Lodges to which the applicants belong, recommending that a Charter be granted to them, the G. W. C. T. and G. Sec. may issue a Charter for a Degree Temple, and arrange for its institution.

SEC. 8. PROPOSITION AND BALLOT.—Candidates for initiation and membership in a Degree Temple must be proposed and recommended by two full Degree members of the Lodge to which they belong, one of whom shall be the W. C. T., P. W. C. T. or Lodge Deputy. The proposition shall be in writing, stating name, residence, occupation, and date when the previous degree was taken. A ballot shall be had when the Temple is open in the degree applied for, and if not more than one black ballot is cast, the candidate shall be declared elected, but if two or more black ballots are cast, the proposition shall then be referred to a committee of three, who shall investigate and report thereon at the next regular meeting, when another ballot shall be taken, and if not more than two black ballots are cast he shall be elected, but if more than two are cast, he shall stand rejected, and shall not be again proposed within three months after such rejection.

SEC. 9. Full Degree members, not members of any Temple, may be proposed for membership by two full

---

* A dispensation does not do away with the ballot upon the admission of the candidate to the Degrees.

Degree members of the Lodge to which they belong
The proposition shall be read when the Temple is open
in the Third Degree, and a ballot taken thereon, and if
not more than seven black ballots are cast, he shall be
admitted to membership upon signing this Constitution and paying the fees.

SEC. 10. MEETINGS.—Degree Temples shall hold
their regular meetings at such times as may be designated in their By-Laws.

SEC. 11. OFFICERS AND TERMS.—The officers of the
Temple shall be: 1st. Degree Templar; 2d, Degree
Vice Templar; 3d, D. Secretary; 4th, D. F. S.; 5th,
D. Treasurer; 6th, D. Chaplain; 7th, D. Marshal; 8th,
D. Guard: 9th, D. Sentinel; 10th, A. D. Secretary;
11th, Deputy D. Marshal; 12th, R. S.; 13th, L. S. The
first seven shall be elected, the eighth and ninth appointed by the D. V. T. elect, the others by the officers
they assist. The regular terms shall commence with
February, and the elective officers shall be chosen by
ballot and a majority vote, at the regular meeting in
January, and installed in February. Any full Degree
member of the Temple shall be eligible to office, but
after the first election, the Degree Templar shall be a
past or acting W. C. T., Degree Templar, or D. G. W.
C. T.

SEC. 12. Suspension or expulsion in the Sub Lodge
shall work a suspension or expulsion from the Temple. No member shall be permitted to take part in
the transactions of the Temple whose dues are unpaid
for the current term, and no person shall be permitted
to sit in the Temple, unless in possession of the current
quarterly password and the password of the degree in
which the Temple is open.

SEC. 13. MISCELLANEOUS.—The following named Articles and Sections of the Sub-Lodge Constitution shall
be binding on the Degree Temples and their members,
after making such changes in the phraseology as may
be necessary to adapt them, or either of them, to the
work of Temple, viz.: Articles I, II, VI and X entire; Article III, Sections 4, 6, 7 and 8; Article V,
Sections 3 and 4; Article IX, Section 4.

ARTICLE VIII.—OFFENSES AND TRIALS.

SEC. 1. CHARGES AND COMMITTEE.—Any member who has reason to believe that another has violated any of the laws of the Order, shall present to the W. C. T. a charge against him in writing, specifying the offense ; and the W. C. T., concealing the name of the accuser, shall refer the charge to a committee of three, which he shall appoint. The committee shall forthwith furnish the accused with a copy of the charge, and summon the accused and witnesses to appear before them at such time and place as they may appoint. At the appointed time and place, the committee shall meet and hear the evidence, which they shall reduce to writing, and, if called upon, produce before the Lodge.

SEC. 2. REPORT AND TRIAL.—The committee shall report, recommending some punishment if they find the charge sustained. The report shall be laid upon the table until the next meeting, at which time the accused shall be summoned to appear, and the Lodge shall act upon it. If called for by any member, the evidence offered before the committee shall be read, but no other evidence shall be introduced. The Lodge may, however, re-commit the case, in order that more evidence may be taken. The accused shall have an opportunity to speak in his defense, and shall then retire. The Lodge shall then decide the question, and if they find him guilty, fix on some mode of punishment; after which he shall be notified of the result. The recommendations of the committee may be amended in any manner before final action is taken on them ; provided, however, that in all cases when a member has been found guilty, he shall be punished by expulsion, suspension, fine or reprimand, except in cases of violation of Article II., when re-obligation *may* be considered a punishment at the option of the Lodge.

SEC. 3. ABSENCE OF ACCUSED.—Should the accused fail to appear before the committee or Lodge when summoned, without sending a sufficient excuse, the trial may proceed as if he were present, or he may be punished for contempt.

SEC. 4. WAIVER.—A member against whom charges

have been preferred may, with the consent of the Lodge, waive any of the forms of trial, and if he acknowledge to the committee or the Lodge that he has committed the offense, the Lodge may forthwith proceed to punish.

SEC. 5. VOTES.—All votes under this article shall be by ballot. A two-thirds vote shall be required to find a member guilty, or to determine the punishment.

SEC. 6. VIOLATION OF ARTICLE II.—A member who has violated Article II, shall be declared expelled, unless he again take the obligation in open Lodge, within four weeks from the time when he made the acknowledgment or was found guilty.

ARTICLE IX.—WITHDRAWAL AND CARDS.

SEC. 1. WITHDRAWAL FROM THE ORDER.—Any member who is free from all charges may withdraw from the Order, only by first filing with the Secretary, a written resignation of membership, which shall lie upon the table until the next regular meeting, when the W. C. T. may, without vote of the Lodge, cause the member's name to be stricken from the roll.

SEC. 2. Clearance and Traveling Cards, of the form prescribed by the R. W. G. Lodge, shall be granted to members applying for them, if they are clear from all charges. A Clearance Card shall be valid for one year from its date, and a Traveling Card for the time for which payment of dues shall be made in advance, not exceeding one year.

SEC. 3. EFFECT OF CARDS.—Members holding cards granted by this Lodge are still members of the Order, and subject to the jurisdiction of this Lodge.

SEC. 4. TRAVELING MEMBERS.—Any member desiring to visit this Lodge on a Traveling Card, shall be examined in the ante-room, and shall not be admitted unless he prove himself in the Traveling Password and the work of the Degree in which the Lodge is opened.

ARTICLE X.—BY-LAWS AND AMENDMENTS.

SEC. 1. BY-LAWS.—This Lodge may adopt such By-Laws and Rules of Order as may be deemed advisable, which do not conflict with this Constitution, or the laws, rules and usages of the Order; provided that said By-Laws and Rules, and all amendments thereto, shall first receive the approval of the G. Lodge, or in the interim between sessions, the approval of the G. W. C. Templar.

SEC. 2. AMENDMENTS.---This Constitution shall be altered or amended only by the R. W. G. Lodge, in the manner provided in the Constitution of Grand Lodges.

ORDER OF BUSINESS OF R. W. G. L.

1st. The R. W. G. L. shall meet at —— o'clock, A. M., and adjourn at —— o'clock.

2d. The R. W. G. T. shall take the chair and call the Lodge to order at the time to which it stands adjourned.

3d. Reading and approving the journals of previous meetings.

4th. Reports of Standing Committees.

5th. Reports of Special Committees.

6th. Petitions and Memorials.

7th. Appeals.

8th. Election and Installation of Officers.

9th. Miscellaneous Business and Good of the Order.

RULES OF ORDER.

1. The R. W. G. T. shall decide all questions of Order, subject to an appeal to the G. L.

2. The R. W. G. T. shall appoint all committees, unless otherwise directed by the G L

3. No member shall speak on any question until first seconded and stated by the chair.

4. No member shall speak more than twice on the same question, nor more than ten minutes, without special leave from the Grand Lodge.

5. No member shall be absent from the session of the G. L. without permission of the R. W. G. T.

6. A motion to adjourn shall always be in order and be taken without debate.

Enuma Elish: The Seven Tablets of Creation, Volume One, by L. W. King. ISBN 1-58509-041-7 • 236 pages • 6 x 9 • trade paper • illustrated • $18.95

Enuma Elish: The Seven Tablets of Creation, Volume Two, by L. W. King. ISBN 1-58509-042-5 • 260 pages • 6 x 9 • trade paper • illustrated • $19.95

Enuma Elish, Volumes One and Two: The Seven Tablets of Creation, by L. W. King. Two volumes from above bound as one. ISBN 1-58509-043-3 • 496 pages • 6 x 9 • trade paper • illustrated • $38.90

The Archko Volume: Documents that Claim Proof to the Life, Death, and Resurrection of Christ, by Drs. McIntosh and Twyman. ISBN 1-58509-082-4 • 248 pages • 6 x 9 • trade paper • $20.95

The Lost Language of Symbolism: An Inquiry into the Origin of Certain Letters, Words, Names, Fairy-Tales, Folklore, and Mythologies, by Harold Bayley. ISBN 1-58509-070-0 • 384 pages • 6 x 9 • trade paper • $27.95

The Book of Jasher: A Suppressed Book that was Removed from the Bible, Referred to in Joshua and Second Samuel, translated by Albinus Alcuin (800 AD). ISBN 1-58509-081-6 • 304 pages • 6 x 9 • trade paper • $24.95

The Bible's Most Embarrassing Moments, with an Introduction by Paul Tice. ISBN 1-58509-025-5 • 172 pages • 5 x 8 • trade paper • $14.95

History of the Cross: The Pagan Origin and Idolatrous Adoption and Worship of the Image, by Henry Dana Ward. ISBN 1-58509-056-5 • 104 pages • 6 x 9 • trade paper • illustrated • $11.95

Was Jesus Influenced by Buddhism? A Comparative Study of the Lives and Thoughts of Gautama and Jesus, by Dwight Goddard. ISBN 1-58509-027-1 • 252 pages • 6 x 9 • trade paper • $19.95

History of the Christian Religion to the Year Two Hundred, by Charles B. Waite. ISBN 1-885395-15-9 • 556 pages. • 6 x 9 • hard cover • $25.00

Symbols, Sex, and the Stars, by Ernest Busenbark. ISBN 1-885395-19-1 • 396 pages • 5 1/2 x 8 1/2 • trade paper • $22.95

History of the First Council of Nice: A World's Christian Convention, A.D. 325, by Dean Dudley. ISBN 1-58509-023-9 • 132 pages • 5 1/2 x 8 1/2 • trade paper • $12.95

The World's Sixteen Crucified Saviors, by Kersey Graves. ISBN 1-58509-018-2 • 436 pages • 5 1/2 x 8 1/2 • trade paper • $29.95

Babylonian Influence on the Bible and Popular Beliefs: A Comparative Study of Genesis I.2, by A. Smythe Palmer. ISBN 1-58509-000-X • 124 pages • 6 x 9 • trade paper • $12.95

Biography of Satan: Exposing the Origins of the Devil, by Kersey Graves. ISBN 1-885395-11-6 • 168 pages • 5 1/2 x 8 1/2 • trade paper • $13.95

The Malleus Maleficarum: The Notorious Handbook Once Used to Condemn and Punish "Witches", by Heinrich Kramer and James Sprenger. ISBN 1-58509-098-0 • 332 pages • 6 x 9 • trade paper • $25.95

Crux Ansata: An Indictment of the Roman Catholic Church, by H. G. Wells. ISBN 1-58509-210-X • 160 pages • 6 x 9 • trade paper • $14.95

Emanuel Swedenborg: The Spiritual Columbus, by U.S.E. (William Spear). ISBN 1-58509-096-4 • 208 pages • 6 x 9 • trade paper • $17.95

Dragons and Dragon Lore, by Ernest Ingersoll. ISBN 1-58509-021-2 • 228 pages • 6 x 9 • trade paper • illustrated • $17.95

The Vision of God, by Nicholas of Cusa. ISBN 1-58509-004-2 • 160 pages • 5 x 8 • trade paper • $13.95

The Historical Jesus and the Mythical Christ: Separating Fact From Fiction, by Gerald Massey. ISBN 1-58509-073-5 • 244 pages • 6 x 9 • trade paper • $18.95

Gog and Magog: The Giants in Guildhall; Their Real and Legendary History, with an Account of Other Giants at Home and Abroad, by F.W. Fairholt. ISBN 1-58509-084-0 • 172 pages • 6 x 9 • trade paper • $16.95

The Origin and Evolution of Religion, by Albert Churchward. ISBN 1-58509-078-6 • 504 pages • 6 x 9 • trade paper • $39.95

The Origin of Biblical Traditions, by Albert T. Clay. ISBN 1-58509-065-4 • 220 pages • 5 1/2 x 8 1/2 • trade paper • $17.95

Aryan Sun Myths, by Sarah Elizabeth Titcomb, Introduction by Charles Morris. ISBN 1-58509-069-7 • 192 pages • 6 x 9 • trade paper • $15.95

The Social Record of Christianity, by Joseph McCabe. Includes *The Lies and Fallacies of the Encyclopedia Britannica,* ISBN 1-58509-215-0 • 204 pages • 6 x 9 • trade paper • $17.95

The History of the Christian Religion and Church During the First Three Centuries, by Dr. Augustus Neander. ISBN 1-58509-077-8 • 112 pages • 6 x 9 • trade paper • $12.95

Ancient Symbol Worship: Influence of the Phallic Idea in the Religions of Antiquity, by Hodder M. Westropp and C. Staniland Wake. ISBN 1-58509-048-4 • 120 pages • 6 x 9 • trade paper • illustrated • $12.95

The Gnosis: Or Ancient Wisdom in the Christian Scriptures, by William Kingsland. ISBN 1-58509-047-6 • 232 pages • 6 x 9 • trade paper • $18.95

The Evolution of the Idea of God: An Inquiry into the Origin of Religions, by Grant Allen. ISBN 1-58509-074-3 • 160 pages • 6 x 9 • trade paper • $14.95

Of Heaven and Earth: Essays Presented at the First Sitchin Studies Day, edited by Zecharia Sitchin. ISBN 1-885395-17-5 • 164 pages • 5 1/2 x 8 1/2 • trade paper • illustrated • $14.95

God Games: What Do You Do Forever?, by Neil Freer. ISBN 1-885395-39-6 • 312 pages • 6 x 9 • trade paper • $19.95

Space Travelers and the Genesis of the Human Form: Evidence of Intelligent Contact in the Solar System, by Joan d'Arc. ISBN 1-58509-127-8 • 208 pages • 6 x 9 • trade paper • illustrated • $18.95

Humanity's Extraterrestrial Origins: ET Influences on Humankind's Biological and Cultural Evolution, by Dr. Arthur David Horn with Lynette Mallory-Horn. ISBN 3-931652-31-9 • 373 pages • 6 x 9 • trade paper • $17.00

Past Shock: The Origin of Religion and Its Impact on the Human Soul, by Jack Barranger. ISBN 1-885395-08-6 • 126 pages • 6 x 9 • trade paper • illustrated • $12.95

Flying Serpents and Dragons: The Story of Mankind's Reptilian Past, by R.A. Boulay. ISBN 1-885395-38-8 • 276 pages • 6 x 9 • trade paper • illustrated • $19.95

Triumph of the Human Spirit: The Greatest Achievements of the Human Soul and How Its Power Can Change Your Life, by Paul Tice. ISBN 1-885395-57-4 • 295 pages • 6 x 9 • trade paper • illustrated • $19.95

Mysteries Explored: The Search for Human Origins, UFOs, and Religious Beginnings, by Jack Barranger and Paul Tice. ISBN 1-58509-101-4 • 104 pages • 6 x 9 • trade paper • $12.95

Mushrooms and Mankind: The Impact of Mushrooms on Human Consciousness and Religion, by James Arthur. ISBN 1-58509-151-0 • 103 pages • 6 x 9 • trade paper • $12.95

Vril or Vital Magnetism, with an Introduction by Paul Tice. ISBN 1-58509-030-1 • 124 pages • 5 1/2 x 8 1/2 • trade paper • $12.95

The Odic Force: Letters on Od and Magnetism, by Karl von Reichenbach. ISBN 1-58509-001-8 • 192 pages • 6 x 9 • trade paper • $15.95

The New Revelation: The Coming of a New Spiritual Paradigm, by Arthur Conan Doyle. ISBN 1-58509-220-7 • 124 pages • 6 x 9 • trade paper • $12.95

The Astral World: Its Scenes, Dwellers, and Phenomena, by Swami Panchadasi. ISBN 1-58509-071-9 • 104 pages • 6 x 9 • trade paper • $11.95

Reason and Belief: The Impact of Scientific Discovery on Religious and Spiritual Faith, by Sir Oliver Lodge. ISBN 1-58509-226-6 • 180 pages • 6 x 9 • trade paper • $17.95

William Blake: A Biography, by Basil De Selincourt. ISBN 1-58509-225-8 • 384 pages • 6 x 9 • trade paper • $28.95

The Divine Pymander: And Other Writings of Hermes Trismegistus, translated by John D. Chambers. ISBN 1-58509-046-8 • 196 pages • 6 x 9 • trade paper • $16.95

Theosophy and The Secret Doctrine, by Harriet L. Henderson. Includes *H.P. Blavatsky: An Outline of Her Life,* by Herbert Whyte, ISBN 1-58509-075-1 • 132 pages • 6 x 9 • trade paper • $13.95

The Light of Egypt, Volume One: The Science of the Soul and the Stars, by Thomas H. Burgoyne. ISBN 1-58509-051-4 • 320 pages • 6 x 9 • trade paper • illustrated • $24.95

The Light of Egypt, Volume Two: The Science of the Soul and the Stars, by Thomas H. Burgoyne. ISBN 1-58509-052-2 • 224 pages • 6 x 9 • trade paper • illustrated • $17.95

The Jumping Frog and 18 Other Stories: 19 Unforgettable Mark Twain Stories, by Mark Twain. ISBN 1-58509-200-2 • 128 pages • 6 x 9 • trade paper • $12.95

The Devil's Dictionary: A Guidebook for Cynics, by Ambrose Bierce. ISBN 1-58509-016-6 • 144 pages • 6 x 9 • trade paper • $12.95

The Smoky God: Or The Voyage to the Inner World, by Willis George Emerson. ISBN 1-58509-067-0 • 184 pages • 6 x 9 • trade paper • illustrated • $15.95

A Short History of the World, by H.G. Wells. ISBN 1-58509-211-8 • 320 pages • 6 x 9 • trade paper • $24.95

The Voyages and Discoveries of the Companions of Columbus, by Washington Irving. ISBN 1-58509-500-1 • 352 pages • 6 x 9 • hard cover • $39.95

History of Baalbek, by Michel Alouf. ISBN 1-58509-063-8 • 196 pages • 5 x 8 • trade paper • illustrated • $15.95

Ancient Egyptian Masonry: The Building Craft, by Sommers Clarke and R. Engelback. ISBN 1-58509-059-X • 350 pages • 6 x 9 • trade paper • illustrated • $26.95

That Old Time Religion: The Story of Religious Foundations, by Jordan Maxwell and Paul Tice. ISBN 1-58509-100-6 • 103 pages • 6 x 9 • trade paper • $12.95

Jumpin' Jehovah: Exposing the Atrocities of the Old Testament God, by Paul Tice. ISBN 1-58509-102-2 • 104 pages • 6 x 9 • trade paper • $12.95

The Book of Enoch: A Work of Visionary Revelation and Prophecy, Revealing Divine Secrets and Fantastic Information about Creation, Salvation, Heaven and Hell, translated by R. H. Charles. ISBN 1-58509-019-0 • 152 pages • 5 1/2 x 8 1/2 • trade paper • $13.95

The Book of Enoch: Translated from the Editor's Ethiopic Text and Edited with an Enlarged Introduction, Notes and Indexes, Together with a Reprint of the Greek Fragments, edited by R. H. Charles. ISBN 1-58509-080-8 • 448 pages • 6 x 9 • trade paper • $34.95

The Book of the Secrets of Enoch, translated from the Slavonic by W. R. Morfill. Edited, with Introduction and Notes by R. H. Charles. ISBN 1-58509-020-4 • 148 pages • 5 1/2 x 8 1/2 • trade paper • $13.95

Sun Lore of All Ages: A Survey of Solar Mythology, Folklore, Customs, Worship, Festivals, and Superstition, by William Tyler Olcott. ISBN 1-58509-044-1 • 316 pages • 6 x 9 • trade paper • $24.95

Nature Worship: An Account of Phallic Faiths and Practices Ancient and Modern, by the Author of Phallicism with an Introduction by Tedd St. Rain. ISBN 1-58509-049-2 • 112 pages • 6 x 9 • trade paper • illustrated • $12.95

Life and Religion, by Max Muller. ISBN 1-885395-10-8 • 237 pages • 5 1/2 x 8 1/2 • trade paper • $14.95

Jesus: God, Man, or Myth? An Examination of the Evidence, by Herbert Cutner. ISBN 1-58509-072-7 • 304 pages • 6 x 9 • trade paper • $23.95

Pagan and Christian Creeds: Their Origin and Meaning, by Edward Carpenter. ISBN 1-58509-024-7 • 316 pages • 5 1/2 x 8 1/2 • trade paper • $24.95

The Christ Myth: A Study, by Elizabeth Evans. ISBN 1-58509-037-9 • 136 pages • 6 x 9 • trade paper • $13.95

Popery: Foe of the Church and the Republic, by Joseph F. Van Dyke. ISBN 1-58509-058-1 • 336 pages • 6 x 9 • trade paper • illustrated • $25.95

Career of Religious Ideas, by Hudson Tuttle. ISBN 1-58509-066-2 • 172 pages • 5 x 8 • trade paper • $15.95

Buddhist Suttas: Major Scriptural Writings from Early Buddhism, by T.W. Rhys Davids. ISBN 1-58509-079-4 • 376 pages • 6 x 9 • trade paper • $27.95

Early Buddhism, by T. W. Rhys Davids. Includes **Buddhist Ethics: The Way to Salvation?,** by Paul Tice. ISBN 1-58509-076-X • 112 pages • 6 x 9 • trade paper • $12.95

The Fountain-Head of Religion: A Comparative Study of the Principal Religions of the World and a Manifestation of their Common Origin from the Vedas, by Ganga Prasad. ISBN 1-58509-054-9 • 276 pages • 6 x 9 • trade paper • $22.95

India: What Can It Teach Us?, by Max Muller. ISBN 1-58509-064-6 • 284 pages • 5 1/2 x 8 1/2 • trade paper • $22.95

Matrix of Power: How the World has Been Controlled by Powerful People Without Your Knowledge, by Jordan Maxwell. ISBN 1-58509-120-0 • 104 pages • 6 x 9 • trade paper • $12.95

Cyberculture Counterconspiracy: A Steamshovel Web Reader, Volume One, edited by Kenn Thomas. ISBN 1-58509-125-1 • 180 pages • 6 x 9 • trade paper • illustrated • $16.95

Cyberculture Counterconspiracy: A Steamshovel Web Reader, Volume Two, edited by Kenn Thomas. ISBN 1-58509-126-X • 132 pages • 6 x 9 • trade paper • illustrated • $13.95

Oklahoma City Bombing: The Suppressed Truth, by Jon Rappoport. ISBN 1-885395-22-1 • 112 pages • 5 1/2 x 8 1/2 • trade paper • $12.95

The Protocols of the Learned Elders of Zion, by Victor Marsden. ISBN 1-58509-015-8 • 312 pages • 6 x 9 • trade paper • $24.95

Secret Societies and Subversive Movements, by Nesta H. Webster. ISBN 1-58509-092-1 • 432 pages • 6 x 9 • trade paper • $29.95

The Secret Doctrine of the Rosicrucians, by Magus Incognito. ISBN 1-58509-091-3 • 256 pages • 6 x 9 • trade paper • $20.95

The Origin and Evolution of Freemasonry: Connected with the Origin and Evolution of the Human Race, by Albert Churchward. ISBN 1-58509-029-8 • 240 pages • 6 x 9 • trade paper • $18.95

The Lost Key: An Explanation and Application of Masonic Symbols, by Prentiss Tucker. ISBN 1-58509-050-6 • 192 pages • 6 x 9 • trade paper • illustrated • $15.95

The Character, Claims, and Practical Workings of Freemasonry, by Rev. C.G. Finney. ISBN 1-58509-094-8 • 288 pages • 6 x 9 • trade paper • $22.95

The Secret World Government or "The Hidden Hand": The Unrevealed in History, by Maj.-Gen., Count Cherep-Spiridovich. ISBN 1-58509-093-X • 203 pages • 6 x 9 • trade paper • $17.95

The Magus, Book One: A Complete System of Occult Philosophy, by Francis Barrett. ISBN 1-58509-031-X • 200 pages • 6 x 9 • trade paper • illustrated • $16.95

The Magus, Book Two: A Complete System of Occult Philosophy, by Francis Barrett. ISBN 1-58509-032-8 • 220 pages • 6 x 9 • trade paper • illustrated • $17.95

The Magus, Book One and Two: A Complete System of Occult Philosophy, by Francis Barrett. ISBN 1-58509-033-6 • 420 pages • 6 x 9 • trade paper • illustrated • $34.90

The Key of Solomon The King, by S. Liddell MacGregor Mathers. ISBN 1-58509-022-0 • 152 pages • 6 x 9 • trade paper • illustrated • $12.95

Magic and Mystery in Tibet, by Alexandra David-Neel. ISBN 1-58509-097-2 • 352 pages • 6 x 9 • trade paper • $26.95

The Comte de St. Germain, by I. Cooper Oakley. ISBN 1-58509-068-9 • 280 pages • 6 x 9 • trade paper • illustrated • $22.95

Alchemy Rediscovered and Restored, by A. Cockren. ISBN 1-58509-028-X • 156 pages • 5 1/2 x 8 1/2 • trade paper • $13.95

The 6th and 7th Books of Moses, with an Introduction by Paul Tice. ISBN 1-58509-045-X • 188 pages • 6 x 9 • trade paper • illustrated • $16.95